Studio Visual Steps

Google Nexus Tablet
for SENIORS

Get started quickly with this user friendly tablet

Visual Steps™
www.visualsteps.com

This book has been written using the Visual Steps™ method.
Cover design by Studio Willemien Haagsma bNO

© 2014 Visual Steps
Author: Studio Visual Steps

First printing: January 2014
ISBN 978 90 5905 359 5

Resources used: A number of definitions and explanations of computer terminology are taken over from the *Google Nexus Guide*.

Do you have any questions or suggestions?
Email: info@visualsteps.com

Would you like more information?
www.visualsteps.com

Website for this book:
www.visualsteps.com/nexustablet
Here you can register your book.

Subscribe to the free Visual Steps Newsletter:
www.visualsteps.com/newsletter

Google Nexus Tablet for SENIORS

Table of Contents

Foreword

The Google Nexus tablet is a very user-friendly, portable multimedia device that offers a wide range of possibilities. For instance, sending and receiving email messages, surfing the Internet, planning a trip, or keeping a calendar.

The tablet comes equipped with a large number of standards apps (programs) that you can use for instance, to work with photos, videos and music. You can also share your photos easily with others.

Apart from that, you can search the *Play Store* for many more free and paid apps. There are games, puzzles, newspapers, magazines, fitness exercises and photo editing apps. You can find apps for almost any purpose you can think of.

In this book you will learn to use the main options and functions of this versatile tablet.

I hope you have a lot of fun learning how to work with the Google Nexus tablet!

Emma Schipper
Studio Visual Steps

PS
We welcome your comments and suggestions.
Our email address is: mail@visualsteps.com

Introduction to Visual Steps™

The Visual Steps handbooks and manuals are the best instructional materials available for learning how to work with mobile devices, computers and software applications. Nowhere else will you find better support to help you get started with *Windows*, *Mac OS X*, an iPad or other tablet, an iPhone, the Internet and various software applications.

Properties of the Visual Steps books:
- **Comprehensible contents**
  Addresses the needs of the beginner or intermediate user for a manual written in simple, straight-forward English.
- **Clear structure**
  Precise, easy to follow instructions. The material is broken down into small enough segments to allow for easy absorption.
- **Screen shots of every step**
  Quickly compare what you see on your screen with the screen shots in the book. Pointers and tips guide you when new windows, screens or alert boxes are opened so you always know what to do next.
- **Get started right away**
  All you have to do is have your tablet or computer and your book at hand. Sit some where's comfortable, begin reading and perform the operations as indicated on your own device.
- **Layout**
  The text is printed in a large size font and is clearly legible.

In short, I believe these manuals will be excellent guides for you.

Dr. H. van der Meij
Faculty of Applied Education, Department of Instructional Technology, University of Twente, the Netherlands

Visual Steps Newsletter

All Visual Steps books follow the same methodology: clear and concise step-by-step instructions with screen shots to demonstrate each task.
A complete list of all our books can be found on our website **www.visualsteps.com**
You can also sign up to receive our **free Visual Steps Newsletter**.
In this Newsletter you will receive periodic information by email regarding:
- the latest titles and previously released books;
- special offers, supplemental chapters, tips and free informative booklets.
Also, our Newsletter subscribers may download any of the documents listed on the web page **www.visualsteps.com/info_downloads**
When you subscribe to our Newsletter you can be assured that we will never use your email address for any purpose other than sending you the information as previously described. We will not share this address with any third-party. Each Newsletter also contains a one-click link to unsubscribe.

What You Will Need

To be able to work through this book, you will need a number of things:

A Google Nexus 7 or 10 tablet with Wi-Fi.

The following item will come in handy, but is not a problem if you do not own it. Just skip the relevant exercises.

A computer or laptop to transfer pictures, videos and music.

The Website Accompanying This Book

On the website that accompanies this book, **www.visualsteps.com/nexustablet**, you will find more information about the book. This website will also keep you informed of changes you need to know as a user of the book. This may include information about updates to *Android* among other things. Be sure to visit our website **www.visualsteps.com** from time to time to read about new books and gather other useful information.

How to Use This Book

This book has been written using the Visual Steps™ method. The method is simple: you put the book next to your tablet and perform each task step by step, directly on your own device. With the clear instructions and the multitude of screen shots, you will always know exactly what to do. By working through all the tasks in each chapter, you will gain a full understanding of your tablet. You can also of course, skip a chapter and go to one that suits your needs.

In this Visual Steps™ book, you will see various icons. This is what they mean:

Techniques
These icons indicate an action to be carried out:

 The index finger indicates you need to do something on the tablet's screen, for instance, tap something, or type a text.

 The keyboard icon means you should type something on the keyboard of your tablet or your computer.

 The mouse icon means you should do something on your computer with the mouse.

 The hand icon means you should do something else, for example rotate the tablet or turn it off. The hand can also indicate a series of operations which you learned at an earlier stage.

In some areas of this book additional icons indicate warnings or helpful hints. These will help you avoid mistakes and alert you when you need to make a decision about something.

Help
These icons indicate that extra help is available:

 The arrow icon warns you about something.

 The bandage icon will help you if something has gone wrong.

 Have you forgotten how to do something? The number next to the footsteps tells you where to look it up at the end of the book in the appendix *How Do I Do That Again?*

The following icons indicate general information or tips concerning the tablet.

Extra information

Information boxes are denoted by these icons:

 The book icon gives you extra background information that you can read at your convenience. This extra information is not necessary for working through the book.

 The light bulb icon indicates an extra tip for using the Google Nexus tablet.

Test Your Knowledge

After you have worked through a Visual Steps book, you can test your knowledge online, on the **www.ccforseniors.com** website. By answering a number of multiple choice questions you will be able to test your knowledge of the Google Nexus. If you pass the test, you can also receive a free *Computer Certificate* by email. Participating in the test is **free of charge**. The computer certificate website is a free service from Visual Steps.

For Teachers

The Visual Steps books have been written as self-study guides for individual use. They are also well suited for use in a group or a classroom setting. For this purpose, some of our books come with a free teacher's manual. You can download the available teacher's manuals and additional materials from the website:
www.visualsteps.com/instructor
After you have registered at this website, you can use this service for free.

The Screen Shots

The screen shots in this book indicate which button, file or hyperlink you need to click on your computer or tablet screen. In the instruction text (in **bold** letters) you will see a small image of the item you need to tap or click. The black line will point you to the right place on your screen.

The small screen shots that are printed in this book are not meant to be completely legible all the time. This is not necessary, as you will see these images on your own tablet screen, in real size and fully legible.

Here you see an example of such an instruction text and a screen shot of the item you need to click. The black line indicates where to find this item on your own screen:

In some cases, the screen shot only displays part of the screen. Below you see an example of this:

We would like to emphasize that we **do not intend you** to read the information in all of the screen shots in this book. Always use the screen shots in combination with the display on your Google Nexus tablet screen.

1. The Google Nexus Tablet

The Google Nexus tablet is a manageable, affordable, and powerful tablet. It is developed by *Google* in conjunction with other hardware partners. The Google Nexus has a 7 or 10 inch screen and runs the *Android* operating system. At the moment of writing this book, these tablets were produced by Asus (7 inch tablet) and Samsung (10 inch tablet). There are lots of things you can do with the Google Nexus tablet. You can use it to surf the Internet or read your email. You can also keep a calendar, play games, listen to music, watch videos, and read books, newspapers or magazines. All these functions are executed by *apps* (programs). There is an assortment of standard apps already installed on the tablet. You can add new apps (free and paid) through the *Google Play Store*. This is an online store that offers a large number of apps.

With your tablet you can connect to the Internet through a wireless network (Wi-Fi). Wi-Fi provides access to the Internet up to a distance of 100 meter (about 33 feet), depending on the strength of the router and on your surroundings. Sometimes you can use Wi-Fi directly through an open or public connection, but in many cases the Wi-Fi connection is secured, which means you will need to enter a password first. At the moment of writing this book, only a few Nexus tablets offered the ability to connect to the Internet through a mobile data network.

In this chapter you will get to know the tablet and learn all of the basic operations needed to operate the tablet including the use of the onscreen keyboard.

In this chapter you will learn how to:

- turn on or unlock the tablet;
- set up the tablet;
- use the main components of the tablet;
- perform basic operations on the tablet;
- connect to the Internet through a wireless network (Wi-Fi);
- create a *Google* account;
- update the tablet;
- lock or turn off the tablet.

 Please note:

The tablet is held in a horizontal position (landscape mode) for most of the screen shots used in this book. We recommend you do this also with your own tablet as you perform the actions described in each chapter. Otherwise the image on your tablet will appear slightly different than the screen shot shown. In certain situations we will let you know ahead of time, if the tablet should be held vertically.

Please note:

This book can be used with a Google Nexus 7 and 10. All functions described in this book are based on the Google Nexus 7. If a particular function operates in a different way or is not available on a specific tablet, we will mention this and if applicable, explain the differences.

1.1 Turning On or Unlock the Tablet

The tablet may be turned off, or unlocked. This is how you turn on your tablet in case it has been turned off:

☞ **Press the Power button** ▬▬▬ **until you see the** *Google* **logo, then release the button**

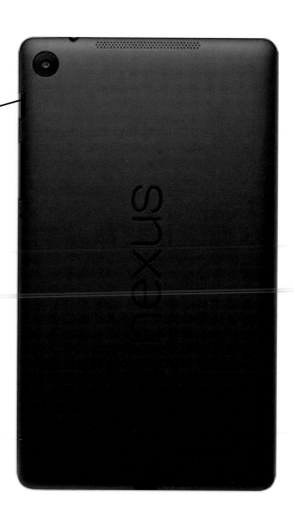

The tablet will be turned on.

Please note: on the Google Nexus 10 tablet you will find the Power button on a other side of the tablet.

The tablet may also be locked. In this case the screen is dark and will not react to any touch gestures. If your tablet is locked, then you can unlock it like this:

☞ **Briefly press the Power button** ▬▬▬

You will still need to unlock the screen:

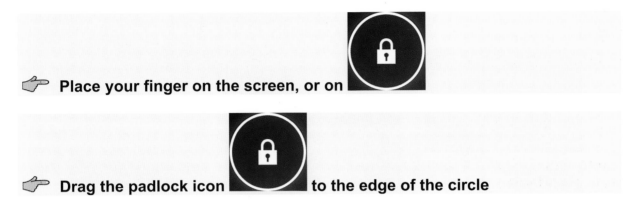

☞ **Place your finger on the screen, or on**

☞ **Drag the padlock icon** **to the edge of the circle**

If this is the first time you turn on your tablet you will first see a couple of screens where you can enter various settings. In the next section you can read how to do this. If you have already used your tablet before you can continue on page 24.

1.2 Setting Up the Tablet

You can set the language used by the tablet.

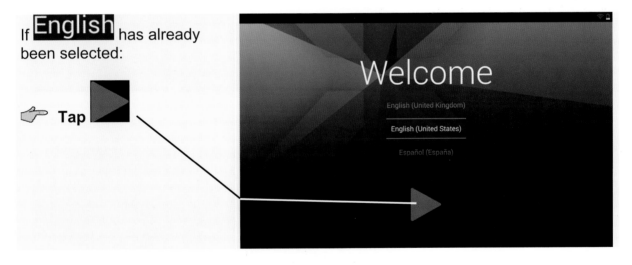

If **English** has already been selected:

☞ **Tap**

If a different language has been selected:

☞ **Drag upwards**

Français (Canada)

Français (France)

Hrvatski

until you see
English

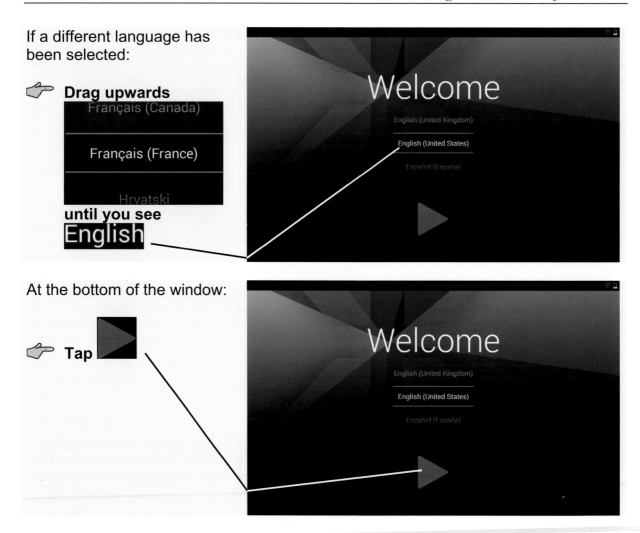

At the bottom of the window:

☞ **Tap**

If you are within reach of a Wi-Fi network you can select this network.

If this is a secure network you will see a small padlock icon next to the network. In that case you need to enter a password:

☞ **Tap the desired Wi-Fi network**

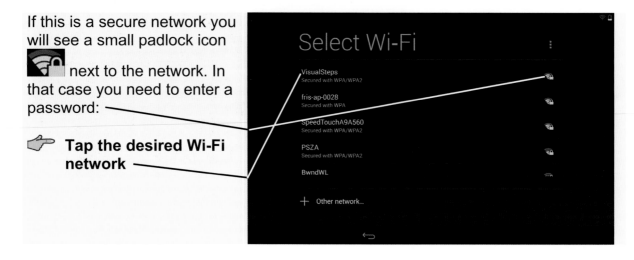

The next action is only required if you are using a secure Wi-Fi network:

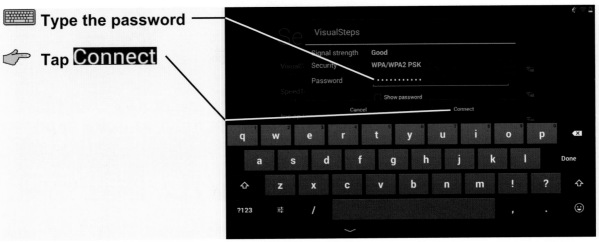

⌨ **Type the password**

☞ **Tap Connect**

💡 **Tip**

Typing on a tablet
On a tablet, you type by gently tapping the letters.

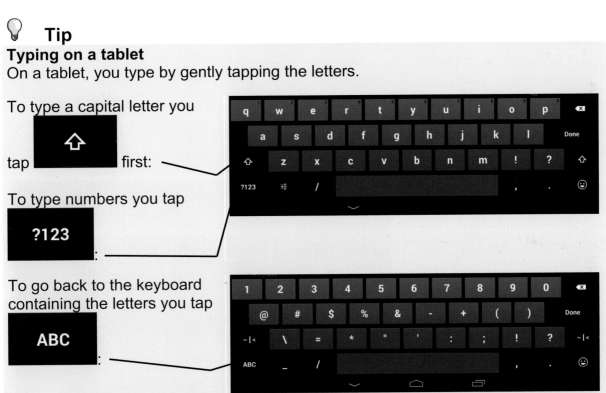

To type a capital letter you

tap ⇧ first:

To type numbers you tap

?123 :

To go back to the keyboard containing the letters you tap

ABC :

You can find more information on typing text on your tablet in *Chapter 2 Email on Your Tablet*.

A connection is established with the Wi-Fi network:

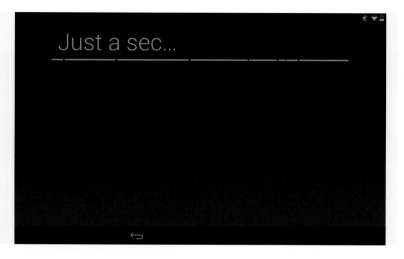

In the next screen you will be asked if you have a *Google* account. Many *Google* and *Android* functions require the use of a *Google* account. A *Google* account is combination of an email address and a password. For the time being you can skip this step. In *section 1.6 Creating and Adding a Google Account* you can read how to create a *Google* account.

 HELP! I see different screens.
You may see different screens on your own tablet. If that is the case, be sure to follow the instructions given in these screens.

☞ Tap No

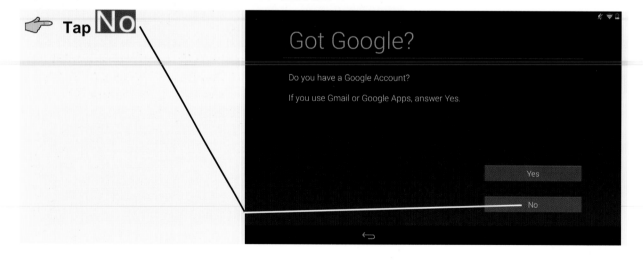

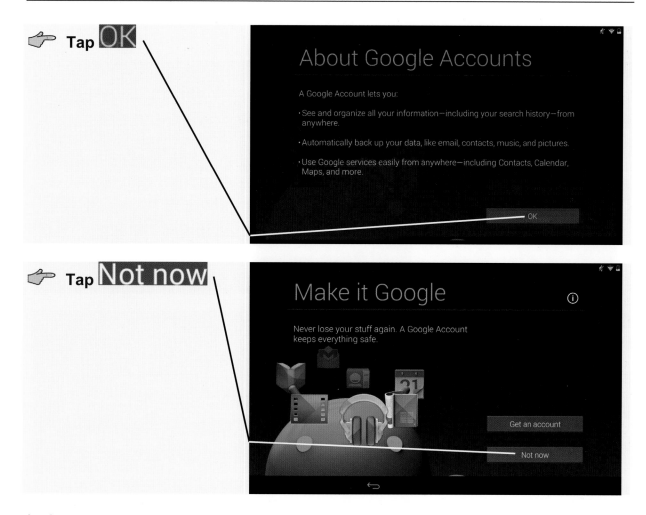

In the next screen you will be asked if you want to use the *Google Location access* function. This function uses Wi-Fi data to determine your geographic location, even when you are not using your tablet. This location information may also be used by other apps, such as *Google Search*. If you do not want to use this function:

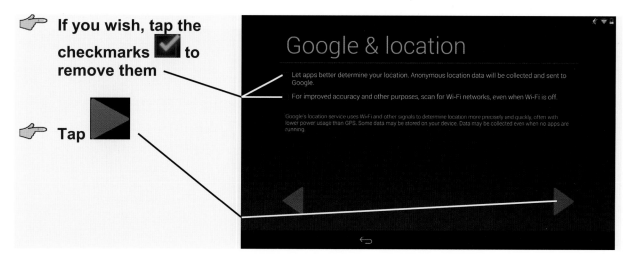

In the next screen you can enter the tablet's owner:

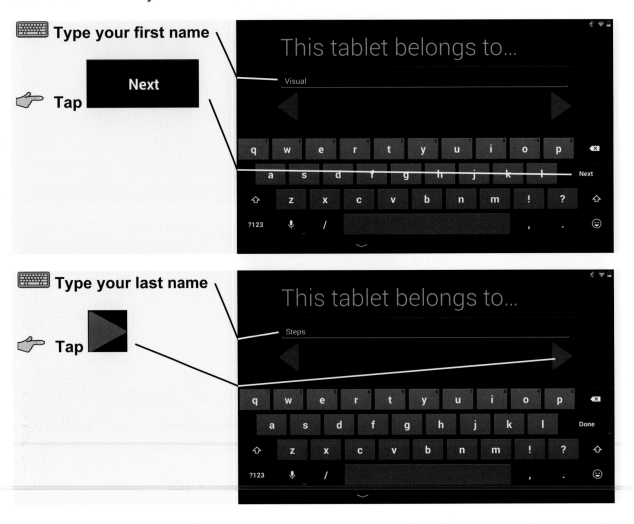

In the next screen you will see a message concerning *Google* services. To accept the terms and conditions:

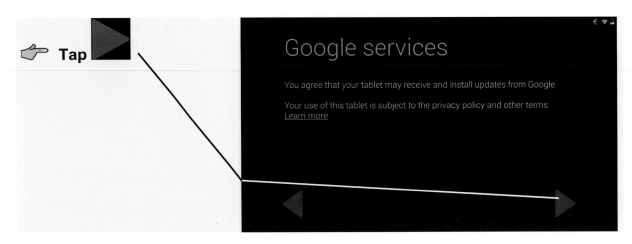

Now the tablet has been set up and is ready for use:

 Tap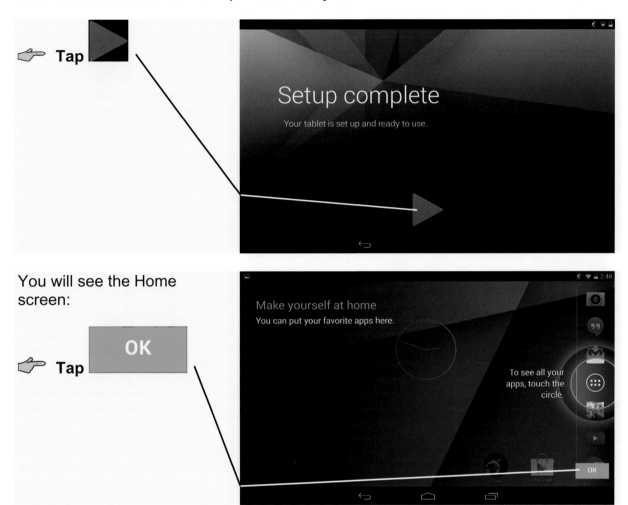

You will see the Home screen:

 Tap **OK**

HELP! My tablet is locked.

If you do not use the tablet for a while it may be locked automatically. This will happen by default, after a pre-set number of seconds. This is how you unlock the tablet:

Press the Power button ▬▬▬

 Drag the padlock icon 🔒 **to the edge of the circle**

1.3 The Main Components of the Google Nexus Tablet

In the images below you can view the main components of the Google Nexus tablet. When we describe how a specific component operates, you can refer back to these images to find its location on the tablet. Here are various views of the tablet:

Google Nexus 7

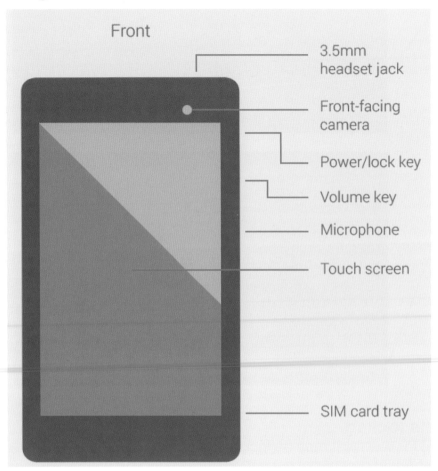

 Tip
Inserting a SIM card
If your tablet has the ability to connect to the Internet through a mobile data network, you will need to insert a SIM card. In the image above, you can see the slot where the SIM card is placed. After insertion, a connection will be made to the data network automatically. You can enable or disable connection to the data network by adjusting the settings.

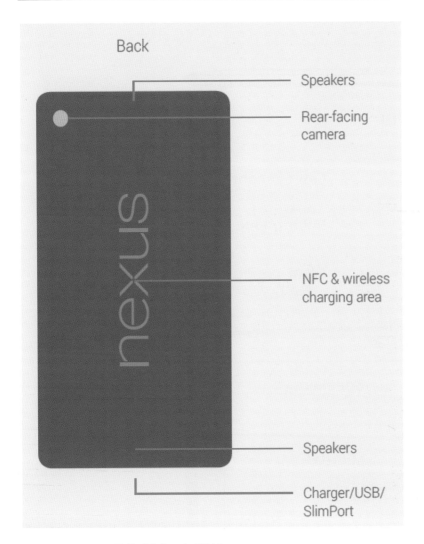

Source: Nexus 7 Guidebook 2013

Google Nexus 10

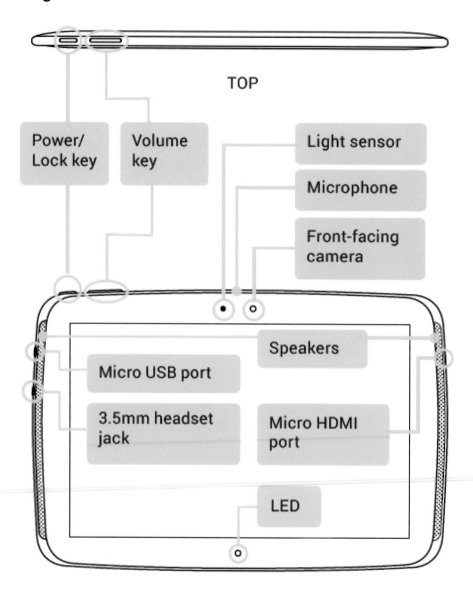

TOP

FRONT

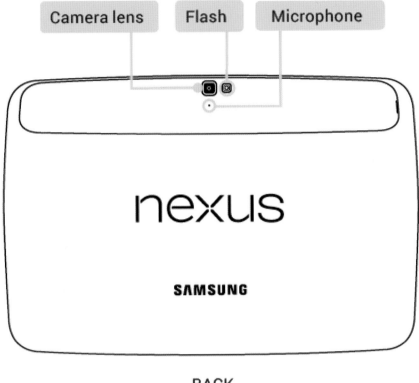

BACK

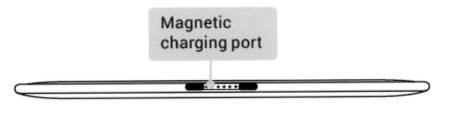

BOTTOM

Source: Nexus 10 Guidebook

This is the Home screen on the Google Nexus tablet:

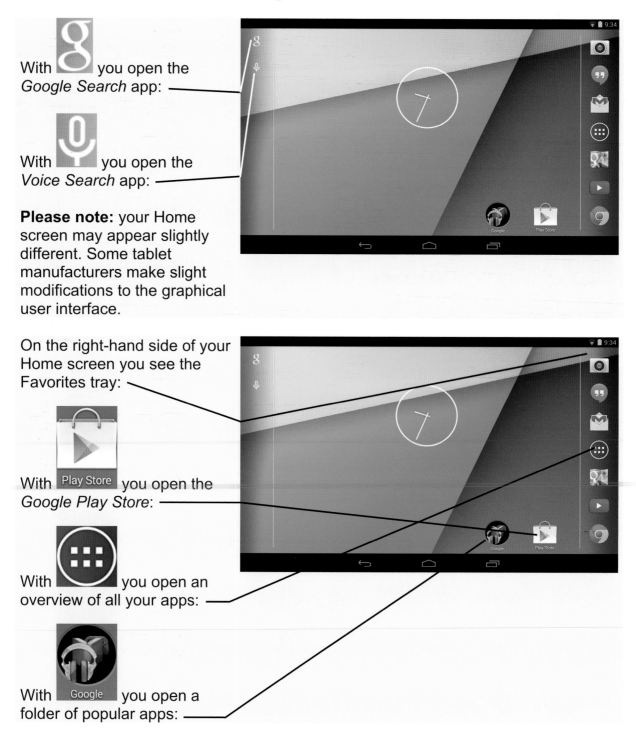

With you open the
Google Search app: ——————

With you open the
Voice Search app: ——————

Please note: your Home
screen may appear slightly
different. Some tablet
manufacturers make slight
modifications to the graphical
user interface.

On the right-hand side of your
Home screen you see the
Favorites tray: ——————

With Play Store you open the
Google Play Store: ——————

With you open an
overview of all your apps: ——————

With Google you open a
folder of popular apps: ——————

At the bottom of the screen you will always see these three navigation buttons: ——

With ⬅ you return to the previous screen:

With 🏠 you go to the Home screen:

With ▭ you open a list of recently used apps:

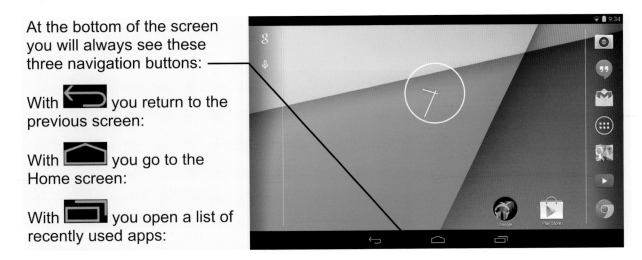

In the top right-hand corner of the screen you will find the system icons (as well as the clock). These icons provide information about the tablet's status and its connections.

📶 indicates the strength of the Wi-Fi connection: ——

🔋 indicates the battery level:

There may be other icons as well, such as 🔵 (Bluetooth enabled) and ✈ (airplane mode enabled).

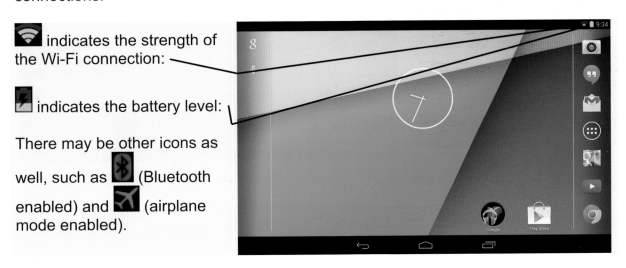

1.4 Basic Tablet Operations

The Google Nexus tablet is easy to operate. In this section you will be practicing some of the basic operations and learn what touch gestures to use. If necessary, unlock the tablet first:

☞ **Unlock the tablet** ¹

You will see the Home screen. You are now going to open the *Quick Settings* window:

☞ **Drag downwards from the top right-hand corner of the screen**

The *Quick Settings* window will appear:

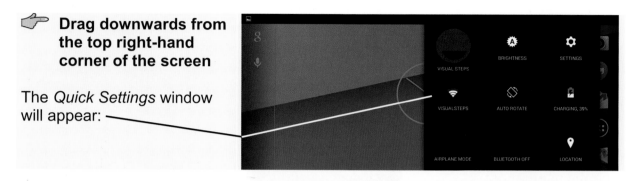

In this window you can quickly adjust a number of settings.

For example, you can lock the screen mode, so the image on the screen will not rotate when you turn the tablet sideways:

☞ Tap AUTO ROTATE

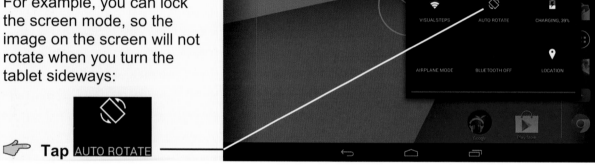

You can test this setting:

☞ **Turn the tablet to a vertical position (portrait mode)**

You will see that the screen orientation does not rotate along with the tablet. It has been locked in landscape mode. If you want to allow the screen to rotate again, then do this:

☞ Tap ROTATION LOCKED

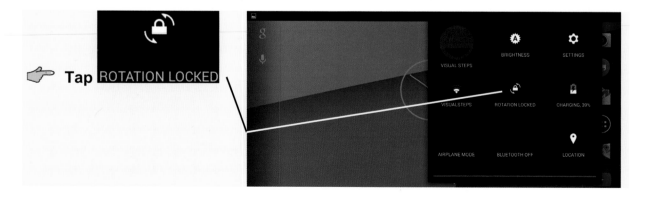

You can also use the *Quick Settings* window to open the *Settings* screen. In the *Settings* screen you can change a large number of tablet settings. For example, you can adjust the sound and display settings and determine the amount of privacy and security you want to use.

To open the *Settings* screen:

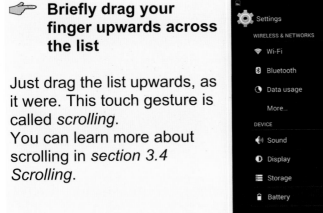

☞ **Tap** SETTINGS

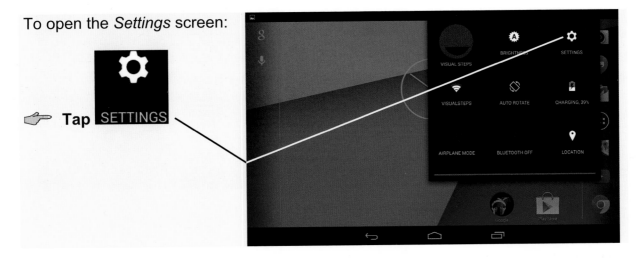

The *Settings* screen contains a large number of icons, more than can be displayed on the screen. Here is how you view the rest of the list:

☞ **Briefly drag your finger upwards across the list**

Just drag the list upwards, as it were. This touch gesture is called *scrolling*.
You can learn more about scrolling in *section 3.4 Scrolling*.

You can scroll the other way round too:

☞ **Drag your finger downwards across the list**

You will see the top of the list again.

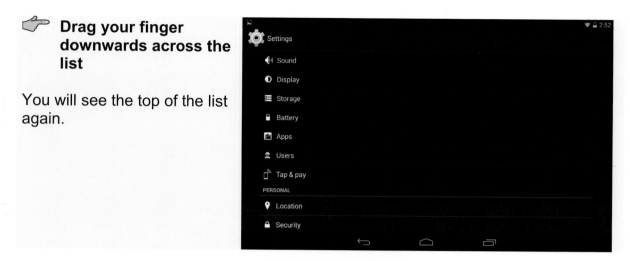

This is how you quit the *Settings* screen and go back to the Home screen:

☞ **Tap** 🏠

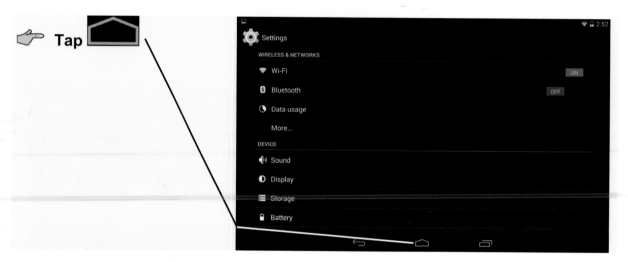

🦅 **Please note:**
The tablet is held in a horizontal position (landscape mode) for most of the screen shots used in this book. We recommend you do this also as you perform the actions described in this chapter. Otherwise the image on your tablet will appear slightly different than the screen shot shown.

1.5 Connect to the Internet using other Wi-Fi networks

Your tablet will connect automatically to the Wi-Fi network you have initially setup for it. But you can also connect to a different Wi-Fi network if you want to use your tablet somewhere else, for instance, at a friend's place or in a bar or hotel. This will only be possible if the Wi-Fi network is currently available and if you know the password, in the case of a secured network.

 Please note:
In the next few steps you will need to have access to another Wi-Fi network. If you do not have such access right now, you can just read through this section.

You can use the *Quick Settings* window to connect to another Wi-Fi network:

☞ **Drag downwards from the top right-hand corner of the screen**

☞ **Tap the name of the Wi-Fi network, in this example**

☞ **Tap the network you want to use**

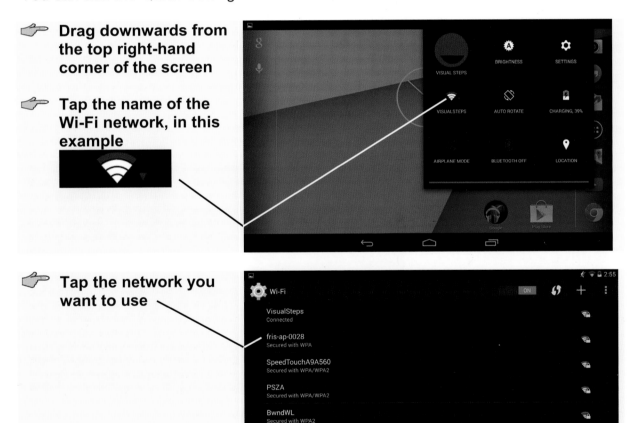

If necessary, tap the password

☞ Tap **Connect**

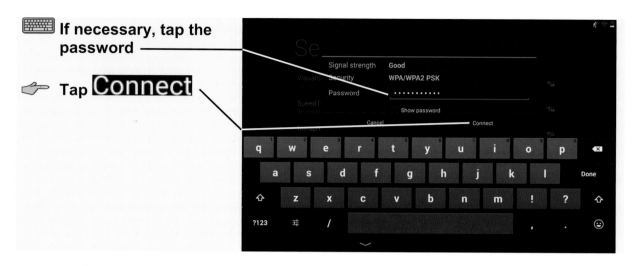

A connection with this wireless network will be established.

☞ **Go back to the Home screen** 🦶²

This is how you disable the connection with a Wi-Fi network:

☞ **Open the *Settings* screen** 🦶³

Here you see the name of the network to which you are connected:

☞ **Drag** ON **to the left until you see** OFF

Now the Wi-Fi connection has been disabled.

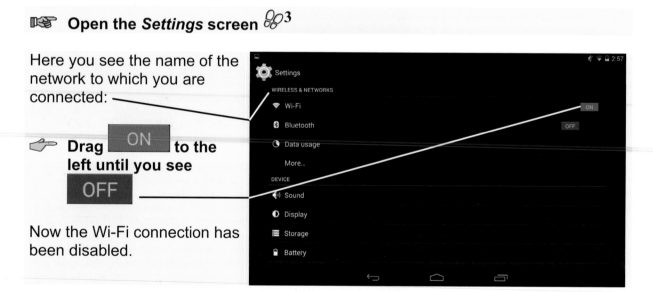

To enable the Wi-Fi
connection once more:

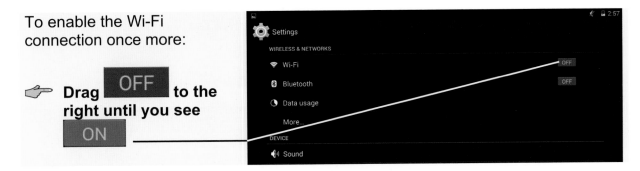

 Drag OFF **to the right until you see** ON

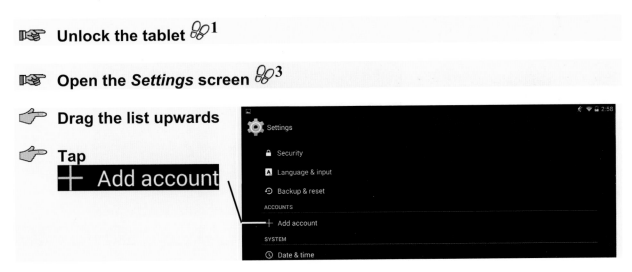

🖐 **Please note:**
If your tablet is able to use a mobile data network, connection will be made automatically to this network when Wi-Fi is not available or has been disabled. You can adjust various settings for data networks of Wi-Fi services in your tablet's settings.

☞ **Go back to the Home screen** 👣**2**

Next time, whenever your tablet is in reach of this particular Wi-Fi network, a connection will be made.

1.6 Creating and Adding a Google Account

Many *Google* and *Android* functions require a *Google* account. A *Google* account is a combination of an email address and a password. In this section you will be creating a new *Google* account. You can use your existing account if you already have one.

☞ **Unlock the tablet** 👣**1**

☞ **Open the *Settings* screen** 👣**3**

☞ **Drag the list upwards**

☞ **Tap** ➕ Add account

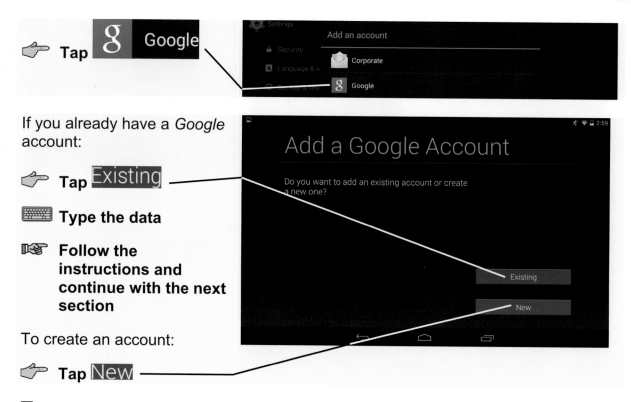

☞ **Tap** **Google**

If you already have a *Google* account:

☞ **Tap Existing**

⌨ **Type the data**

☞ **Follow the instructions and continue with the next section**

To create an account:

☞ **Tap New**

🐾 **Please note:**
Before you start to enter the data for your *Google* account, it is best to turn the tablet to a vertical position (portrait mode). In landscape mode, some of the components may not be visible.

☞ **Hold the tablet in a vertical position**

First, enter your first and last name:

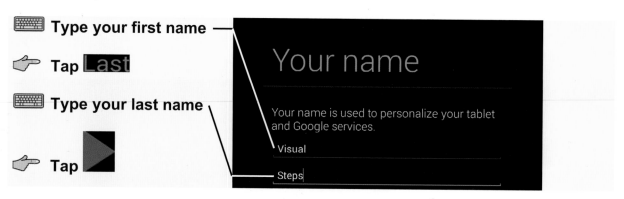

⌨ **Type your first name**

☞ **Tap Last**

⌨ **Type your last name**

☞ **Tap** ▶

✖ **HELP! I see different screens.**
You may see different screens on your own tablet. If that is the case, be sure to follow the instructions given in the screens.

You can choose your own email address. This email address will end in @gmail.com.

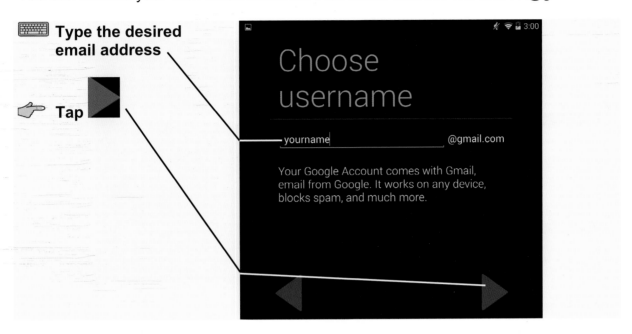

Type the desired email address

 Tap ▶

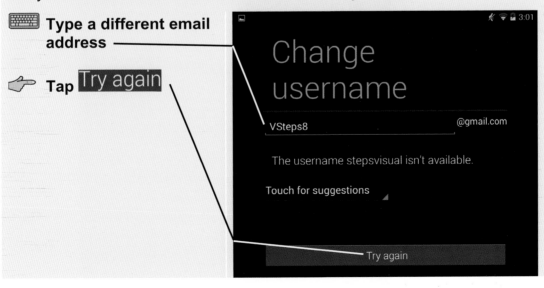

✖ HELP! The email address is already in use.

If the email address you have typed is already being used by someone else, you will see this message: The username stepsvisual isn't available.

If you wish, you can select one of the suggestions presented by *Google*. First, tap Touch for suggestions and then tap one of the suggestions.

But you can also enter a different email address yourself:

Type a different email address

 Tap Try again

The password that goes with your *Google* account needs to consist of at least eight characters:

Type the desired password ────────────

☞ **Tap** `Re-type password`

Re-type the password

At the bottom of the screen:

☞ **Tap** ◨

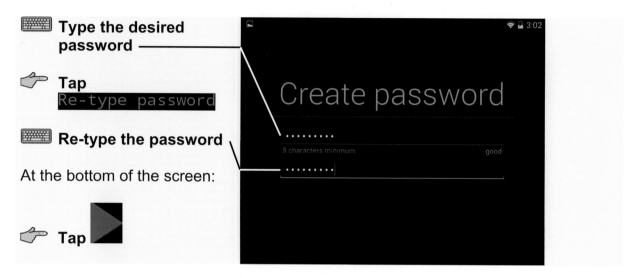

You will see a screen about password recovery:

☞ **Tap** Not now ──────

If you want to, tap Set up recovery options and follow the instructions.

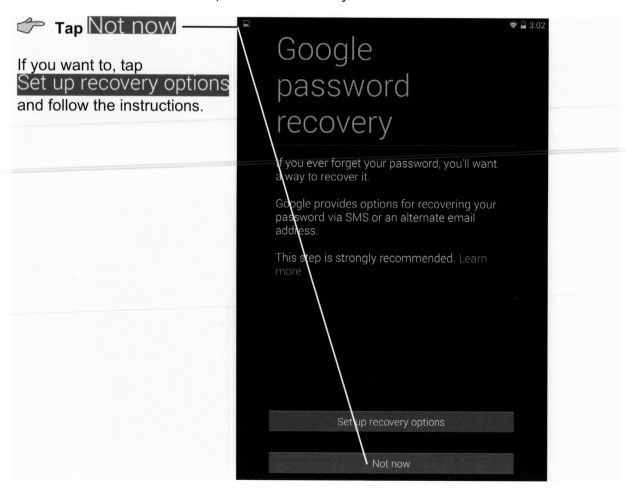

You will see a screen with information on creating backups:

At the bottom of the screen:

 **Tap**

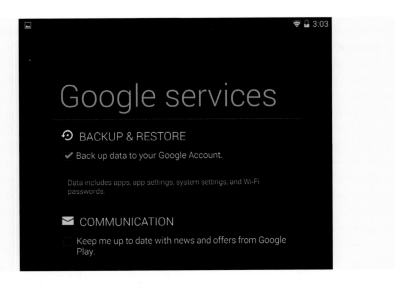

In order to continue you will need to agree to the terms and conditions and the privacy policy stated by *Google*:

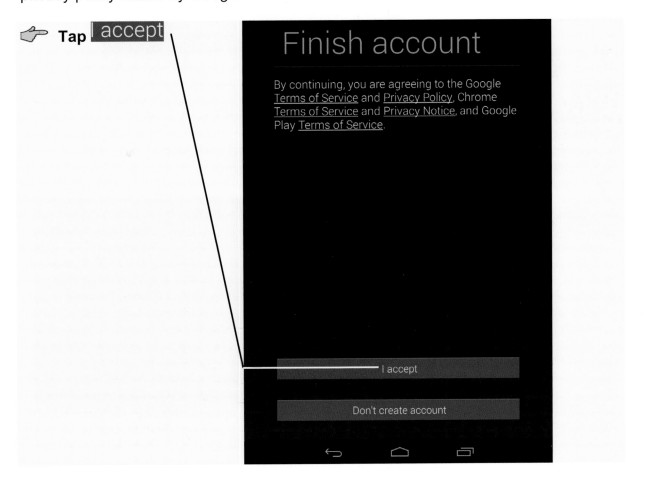

Tap **accept**

You will see a text box with some characters you need to copy:

Type the text you see in the white box

Tap

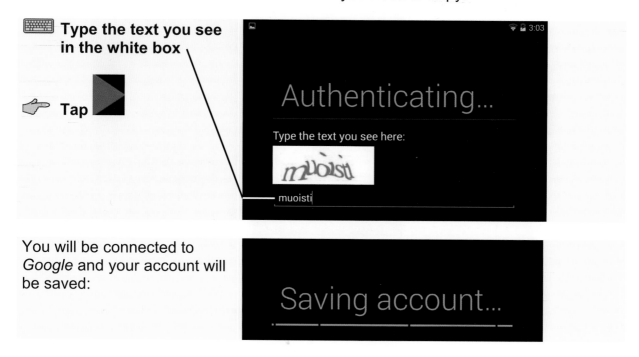

You will be connected to *Google* and your account will be saved:

Turn the tablet sideways again:

Hold the tablet in a horizontal position

You will be asked if you want to use *Google+*. This is the social network site from *Google*. It is comparable to *Facebook*. For now this will not be necessary:

Tap Not now

Your *Google* account has been added to your tablet. You can now go back to the Home screen:

Go back to the Home screen $\mathcal{QQ}$2

1.7 Manually Updating the Google Nexus Tablet

Every time new software becomes available for the Google Nexus tablet, you will receive a notification message which you can accept. If you want to check the availability of new updates manually, you can do that like this:

☞ **Unlock the tablet** 🐾¹

☞ **Open the *Settings* screen** 🐾³

👉 **Drag the list downwards**

👉 **Tap ⓘ About tablet**

👉 **Tap System updates**

👉 **Tap Check now**

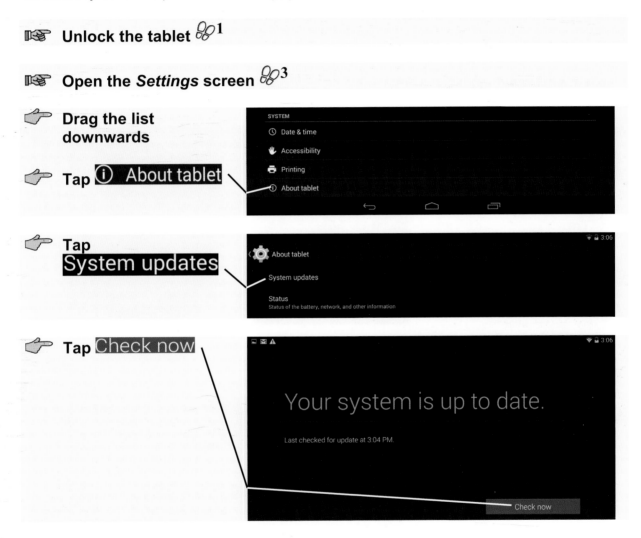

If any new software is available you will now be able to install it.

☞ **If necessary, follow the instructions on the screens**

↘ **Please note:**

Updates can be large in scale and require additional time to download and install. It is therefore best to do an update when a Wi-Fi connection is available rather than incur the extra costs that may be applied using a mobile data network.

1.8 Lock or Turn Off the Tablet

When you stop using the tablet you can lock it or turn it off completely. If you lock it the tablet will still be turned on but consume less energy. If you have turned off Wi-Fi, the tablet will hardly use any energy at all. This is how you lock the tablet:

☞ **Briefly press the Power button** ▭▭▭

The screen will turn off and will no longer react to touch gestures.

If you want to turn off the tablet completely, you do the following:

☞ **Tap and hold the Power button** ▭▭▭ **pressed down until you see this screen**

☞ **Tap** ⏻ **Power off**

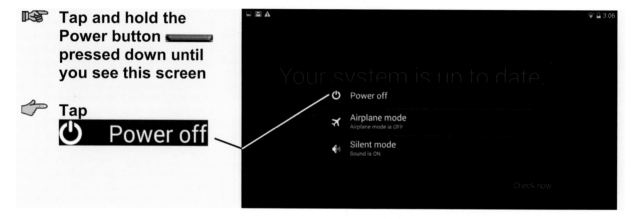

You will need to confirm this action:

☞ **Tap** **OK**

The tablet is turned off. In future, you can decide for yourself whether you want to lock or turn off the tablet.

In this chapter you have become acquainted with the main components and basic operations of the Google Nexus tablet. In the *Background Information* and the *Tips* you will find additional information.

1.9 Background Information

Dictionary

Android	A mobile operating system for mobile phones (smartphones), tablets and other devices. *Android* is not connected to a single specific manufacturer. *Google* provides a free *Android* version to various manufacturers of mobile devices. Many smartphone and tablet manufacturers may modify the user interface of their devices. This can cause significant differences in the 'look and feel' and operation of these devices even if they use the same version of *Android*.
App	Short for *application*, a program for the tablet.
Dock station/ docking station	A device in which you can place your tablet in order to charge the batteries, or to listen to music. This is an optional accessory item and is not included with your tablet.
Favorites tray	On the Home screen you can find the Favorites tray. This quickly brings you to your apps, music, etcetera.
Google account	Combination of a user name and a password that provides access to the *Google* and *Android* functions and services.
Google Nexus tablet	The Google Nexus tablet is a portable multimedia device (a tablet computer) co-developed by *Google* and *Asus*. It features a touch screen and runs the *Android* operating system.
Home screen	The screen that you see when you turn on or unlock the tablet.
Lock	You can lock the tablet if you no longer want to use it by turning off the screen with the Power button. Once the tablet has been locked it will no longer react to touch gestures.
Lock screen	The screen that you see when you turn on the tablet after it has been locked. You will need to unlock the lock screen before you can use the tablet.
Play Store	An online store where you can download free and paid apps.
Power button	The button ▬ with which you can lock, unlock, turn on or turn off the tablet.

- Continue on the next page -

Sleep mode   A function that will turn off and lock the tablet after a few moments of inactivity. The amount of time that elapses before Sleep mode starts can be adjusted in the display settings.

Tablet, tablet PC   A tablet is a computer that does not have a casing or a separate keyboard. It is usually operated by a touch screen or pen-enabled interface.

Wi-Fi   A wireless Internet network.

Source: Google Nexus tablet Guidebook, Wikipedia

The Android operating system

Android is a mobile operating system for mobile phones (smartphones), tablets and other devices. It was originally developed by Android Inc., a company that was bought by *Google* in 2005. *Android* is not bound to a single specific manufacturer, as is the case with the *iOS* operating system manufactured by *Apple*. *Google* allows manufacturers of mobile devices to use the *Android* operating system for free.

New versions of *Android* are continuously being released. During the developing stage the new versions are given a code name that is often based on a well-known type of dessert or candy. The first letters of these code names are placed in alphabetical order:

- 1.5 Cupcake;
- 1.6 Donut;
- 2.0/2.1 Eclair;
- 2.2 Frozen Yoghurt /FroYo;
- 2.3 Gingerbread;
- 3.1/3.2 Honeycomb;
- 4.0 Ice Cream Sandwich;
- 4.1/4.2/4.3 Jelly Bean;
- 4.4 KitKat.

Many manufacturers of smartphones and tablets do not use the standard *Android* user interface on their devices. They often develop their own user interface instead. This will cause the tablets of different manufacturers to look and function differently, even though they use the same version of the *Android* operating system.

1.10 Tips

 Tip

Sleep mode

Your tablet is set by default to lock automatically after two minutes of inactivity. This setting does saves battery energy. But you may want to allow your tablet to stay active a little while longer. You can adjust these settings yourself:

☞ **Open the *Settings* screen** 🐾³

👉 **Tap** ⚙ **Display**

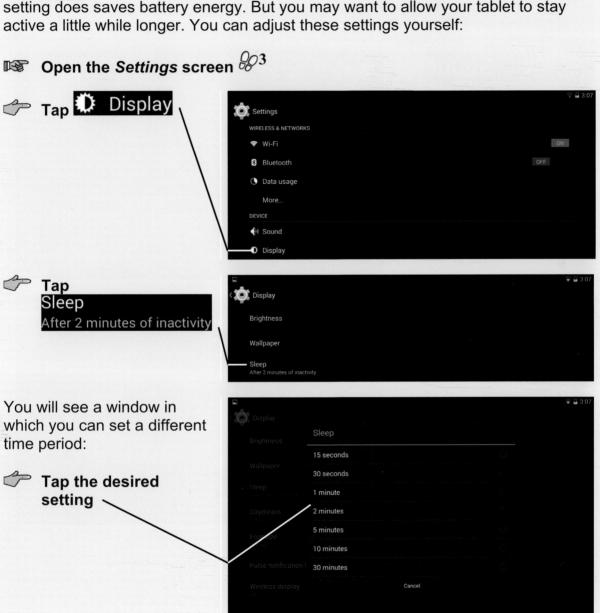

👉 **Tap**
Sleep
After 2 minutes of inactivity

You will see a window in which you can set a different time period:

👉 **Tap the desired setting**

Tip

Setting sounds

Your tablet will use various sounds for different events, for example, when you receive an email or a notification, or when you use the keyboard. You can select which sounds you do and do not want to hear. You do this in the *Settings* screen:

☞ **Open the *Settings* screen** 🐾³

☞ **Tap**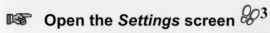

Here you can change the default sound for notifications: ────────

You can also enable or disable the sounds that go with touching the screen, locking the screen, and placing the tablet in a docking station:

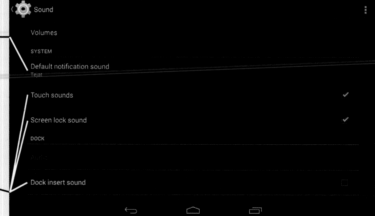

💡 Tip

Secure with a pattern

Your tablet is protected by default from accidental input operations. When you turn on the tablet, you usually drag the padlock to the edge of the circle, in order to unlock it. This operation can just as easily be performed by anyone else. You can take additional measures to make your tablet more secure, by using a PIN code, a password, or a pattern. Here is how you do that:

☞ **Open the *Settings* screen** ✍³

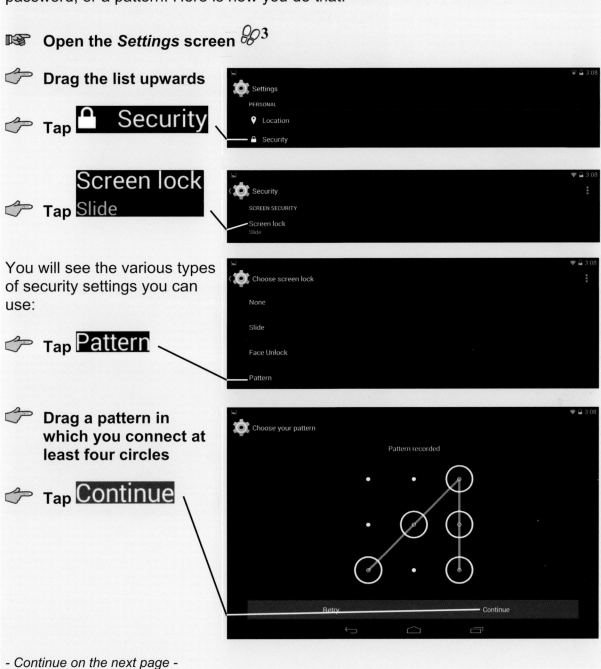

☞ **Drag the list upwards**

☞ **Tap** 🔒 **Security**

☞ **Tap Screen lock Slide**

You will see the various types of security settings you can use:

☞ **Tap Pattern**

☞ **Drag a pattern in which you connect at least four circles**

☞ **Tap Continue**

- Continue on the next page -

☞ **Drag the same pattern once again**

☞ **Tap Confirm**

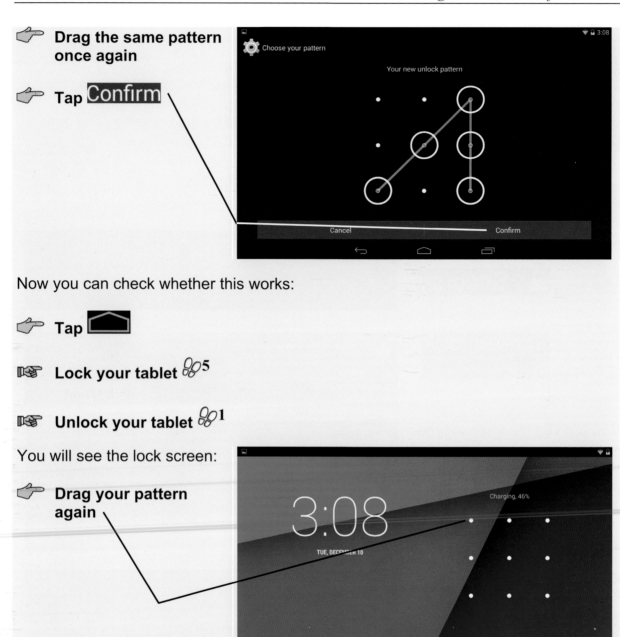

Now you can check whether this works:

☞ **Tap** ⬛

☞ **Lock your tablet** 👣⁵

☞ **Unlock your tablet** 👣¹

You will see the lock screen:

☞ **Drag your pattern again**

2. Email on Your Tablet

Your Google Nexus tablet comes with two standard apps for sending and receiving email messages: *Gmail* and *Email*. The *Gmail* app has been developed for accounts that use *Google's* web-based email service known as *Gmail*. In the *Email* app you can also manage emails sent by other providers.
Both apps will let you write, send, and receive email messages just like you do on a regular desktop computer.

In this chapter you will read how to use the *Email* app. First you need to add an email account so you can start working with the app.

It is very easy to write email messages with your tablet. In this chapter you will practice sending, receiving, and deleting email. You will learn how to type text, numbers, and special characters using the onscreen keyboard. We also explain how to select, copy, cut and paste text. And finally, we show you how to use the auto-correct function.

In this chapter you will learn how to:

- set up an email account in the *Email* app;
- write en send an email;
- receive an email;
- move an email to the *Trash* folder;
- permanently delete an email.

 Tip

Gmail
If you use *Gmail* you can also use the *Gmail* app instead of the *Email* app. The *Gmail* app works pretty much the same as the *Email* app.

2.1 Adding an Email Account in the Email App

In this section you are going to open the *Email* app and learn how to add an email account for an Internet or email service provider, such as Charter, Comcast, Cox, AT & T, EarthLink or Verizon. For this you will need to have the server data, username, and password given to you by your service provider. If you are using a web-based email service and have an email address that ends in hotmail.com, outlook.com, live.com, or gmail.com, you can set up these accounts too.

☞ **Unlock or turn on the tablet** $\mathscr{C\!\!\!C}^1$

You open the *Email* app from the screen showing an overview of all the apps:

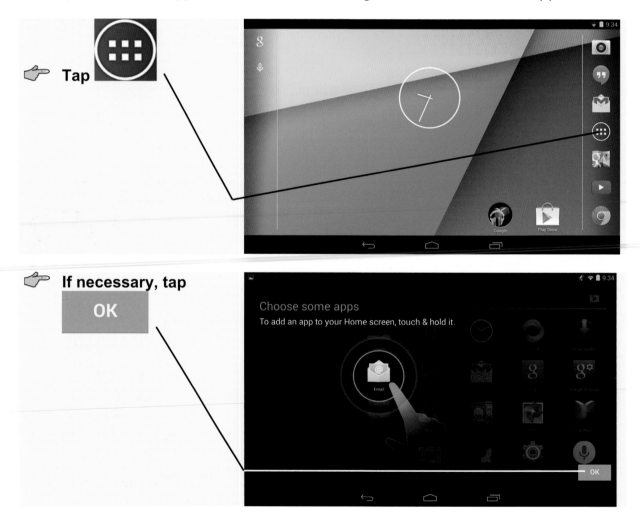

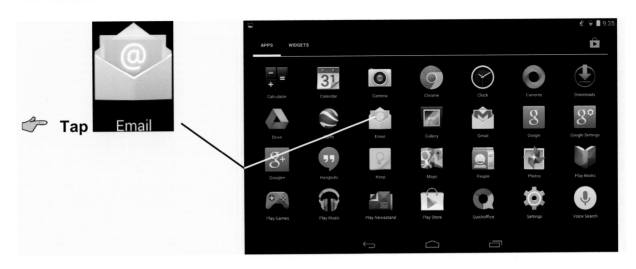

👉 **Tap** Email

You will see a screen where you need to enter some basic information concerning your email account. You can use the onscreen keyboard to enter the data:

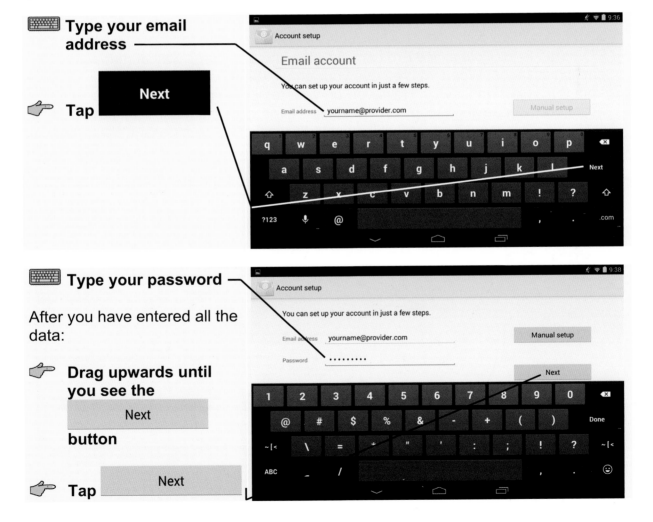

⌨ **Type your email address**

👉 **Tap** Next

⌨ **Type your password**

After you have entered all the data:

👉 **Drag upwards until you see the** Next **button**

👉 **Tap** Next

Please note:

If you use an email address that ends in *live.com*, *hotmail.com* or *gmail.com*, you can skip the next couple of steps. You will just see a screen with account options, and a screen in which you can edit the account name. Afterwards the account will be created automatically. If this is the case, then continue on page 54.

Now you can choose how you want to set up your email account: as an *IMAP* or as a *POP* account:

- IMAP stands for *Internet Message Access Protocol*. This means that you manage your email messages on the mail server. Messages that have been read will still be stored on the mail server until you delete them. IMAP is useful if you want to manage your emails from multiple computers or devices. Your mailbox will look exactly the same on all of your devices. If you have created folders to arrange your email messages, these folders will be available on each computer you use and on your tablet too. If you want to use IMAP you will need to set up your email account as an IMAP account on each device you use.

- POP stands for *Post Office Protocol*, which is the traditional way of managing email messages. When you retrieve your email, the messages are usually deleted from the server right away. However, on your tablet the default setting for POP accounts is for saving a copy on the server, even after the messages have been retrieved. This means you will still be able to receive these messages on your computer later on.

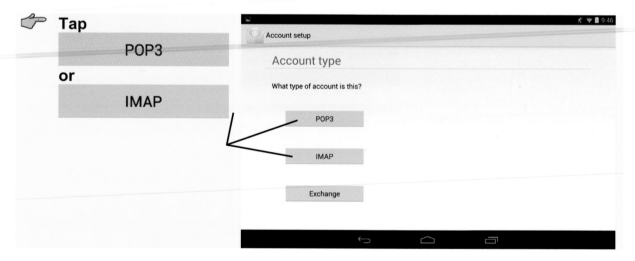

Now you can enter the data sent to you by your email service provider:

By Username, type your username

If necessary, type your password by Password

Drag upwards until you see the rest of the list

By Server, type the name of the incoming mail server

Tap
Next

By SMTP server, type the name of the outgoing mail server

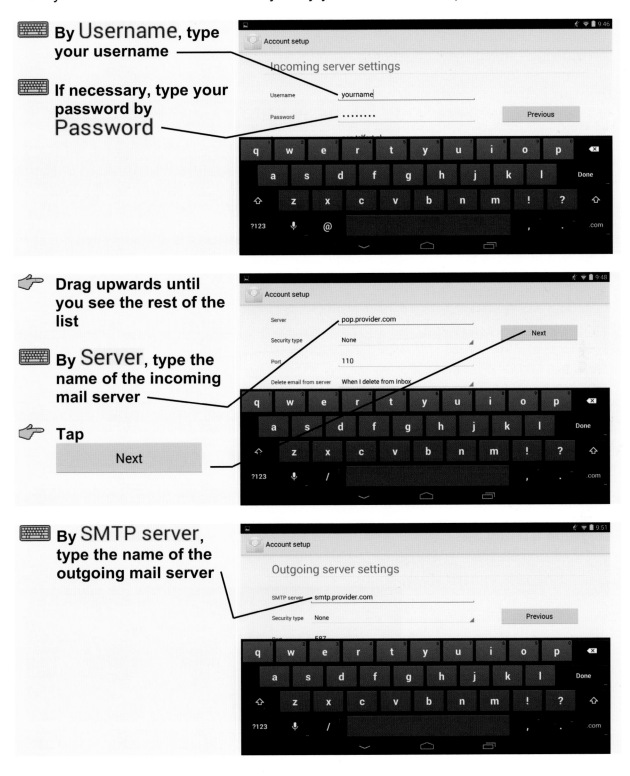

☞ **Drag upwards until you see the** Next **button**

☞ **Tap** Next

You will see this screen:

☞ **Tap** Next

If you wish:

⌨ **Type a name by** Give this account a name

☞ **Drag upwards until you see** Your name

⌨ **Type a different name by** Your name, **if you wish**

☞ **Tap**

Next

You may see the screen showing all the apps:

☞ **If necessary, tap**

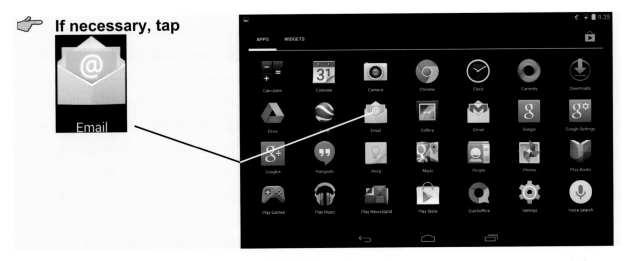

Now you will see the screen of the *Email* app:

In this example we have not yet received any messages.

You may see one or more messages on your own tablet.

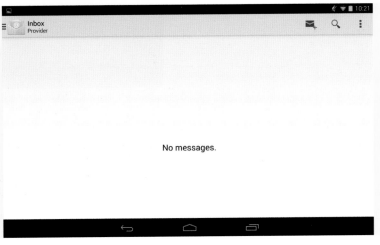

2.2 Writing and Sending an Email Message

To practice, you are going to write and send an email message to yourself. Open a new, blank email:

In the top right-hand corner of the screen:

☞ **Tap**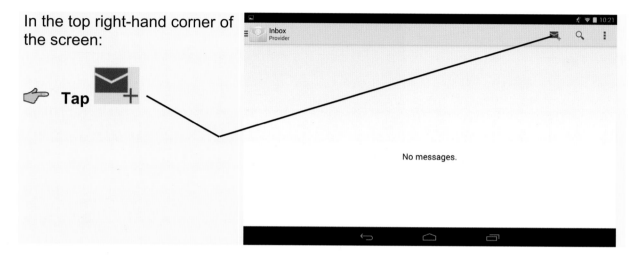

A new message is opened.

⌨ **By** To**, type your email address**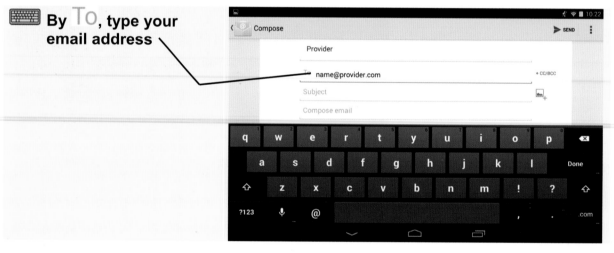

💡 **Tip**
Contacts
If contacts have already been added to the *People* app, you will see a list of names with corresponding email addresses as soon as you have typed the first two letters of a name. You can quickly add the email address by tapping the desired name.
In *Chapter 4 The Standard Apps on Your Google Nexus Tablet* you will learn how to manage your list of contacts in the *People* app.

☞ **Tap** Subject

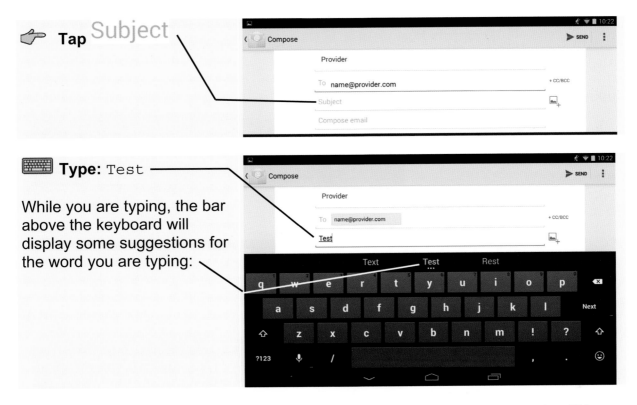

⌨ **Type:** Test

While you are typing, the bar above the keyboard will display some suggestions for the word you are typing:

This function is called *Word Prediction*. While you are typing, several words will be suggested on the basis of the letters you just typed. This may save you a lot of typing. The best suggestion is placed in the middle. You can accept this suggestion by tapping the space bar. The other suggestions can be accepted by simply tapping them. Just try this with the first part of the word 'computer'.

☞ **Drag upwards until you see** Compose email

☞ **Tap** Compose email

Type: Compu

In the middle you will see the suggested word **Computer**:

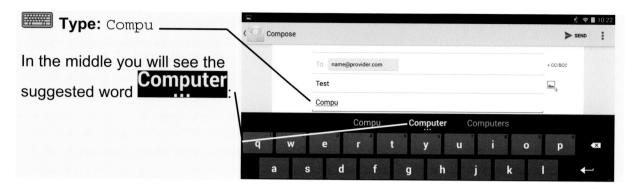

To accept the suggestion:

☞ **Tap the space bar**

'Compu' has been replaced by 'Computer':

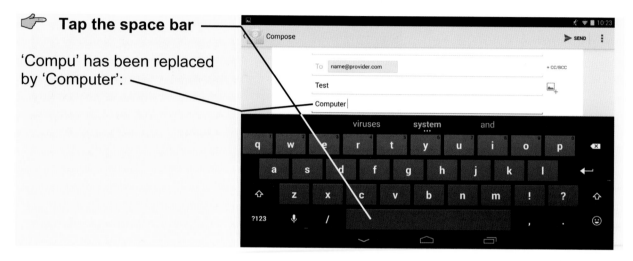

The nice thing about this function is its ability to automatically correct lots of spelling errors at the same time. Just see what happens if you make a spelling mistake on purpose:

☞ **Tap** ⬅

Type: Screene

You see that the word **Screen** is the best suggestion:

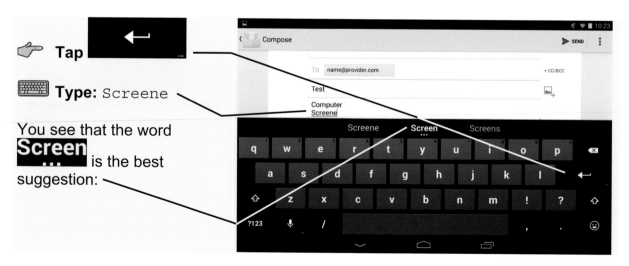

Accept the suggestion by tapping the space bar or Enter , right after the word. Your mistake will be corrected. You may not even notice you have made a mistake.

 **Tap the space bar**

The word 'Screen' has now been inserted in the text:

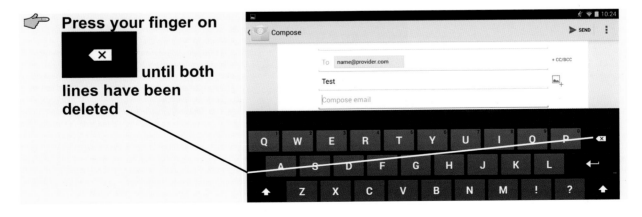

 Tip

Accept correction
A suggested correction will also be accepted if you type a period, comma, or any other punctuation mark.

Tip

Select your own entry or a different suggestion
If the word that is suggested is incorrect, you can select the text you have entered yourself in the email message by tapping it. You can do the same thing with the suggestions that are not placed in the middle.

Tip

Disable Word Prediction
In the *Tips* at the end of this chapter you can read how to disable the *Word Prediction* function while you are typing.

If you are not satisfied with the text you have typed, you can delete it with the Backspace key:

Press your finger on

until both lines have been deleted

The first letter in a sentence will automatically be a capital letter. If you want to type capitals or exclamation marks in the middle of a sentence, you tap .

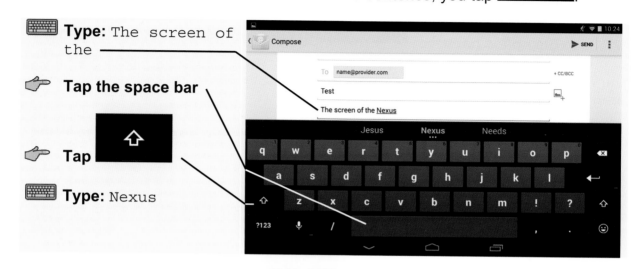

Type: The screen of the

☞ **Tap the space bar**

☞ **Tap**

Type: Nexus

To type numbers you need to tap . To go back to the letters on the keyboard, just tap ABC again.

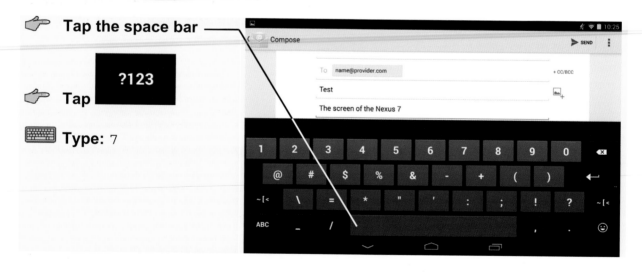

☞ **Tap the space bar**

☞ **Tap** ?123

Type: 7

☞ **Tap the space bar** ——

 Type: `tablet is touch sensitive!`

💡 **Tip**

Unknown word
If the word is unknown and no word predictions have been found, the word will be underlined in red.

☞ **Tap the word underlined in red**

You will still see some suggestions for the word. You can also decide to add the word to the dictionary, if you like, or simply delete the word.

In the *Email* app you can also copy, cut, and paste text. You can do this with a single word, multiple words, or an entire text at once. In this example we will be using a single word. This is how you select a word:

☞ **Press your finger on the word** Nexus ——

The word will be selected and you will see blue handles (tabs) below the word:

☞ **Release your finger from the screen**

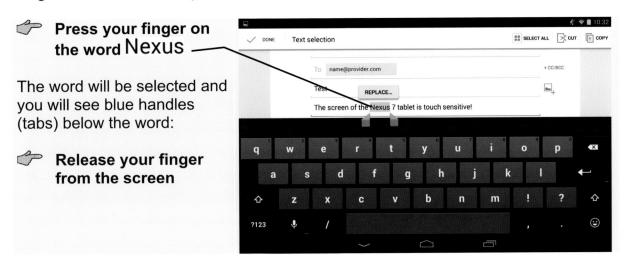

By using the tabs you can change the selection. Practice now by selecting the text 'Nexus 7 tablet':

☞ **Drag the right-hand**

tab ▄ **across**
7 tablet

Now the full name has been selected:

You can cut, copy, or replace the selected words. You are going to copy the words:

☞ **Tap** 📋 **COPY**

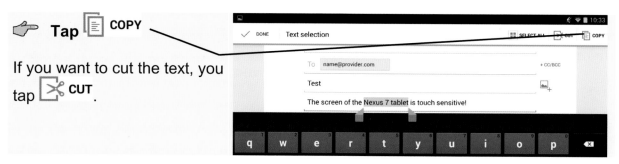

If you want to cut the text, you tap ✂ **CUT**.

The words have been copied to the clipboard. This is how you paste them into the text:

☞ **Tap next to the text, on the right-hand side**

☞ **Tap** ⬅

twice

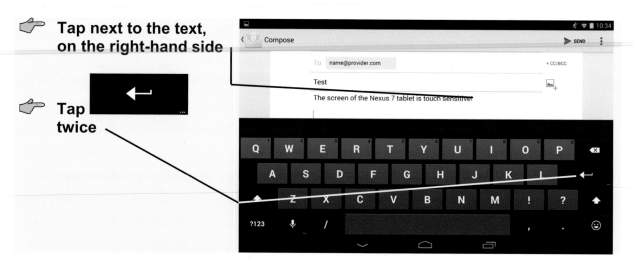

Tap below the text

Tap

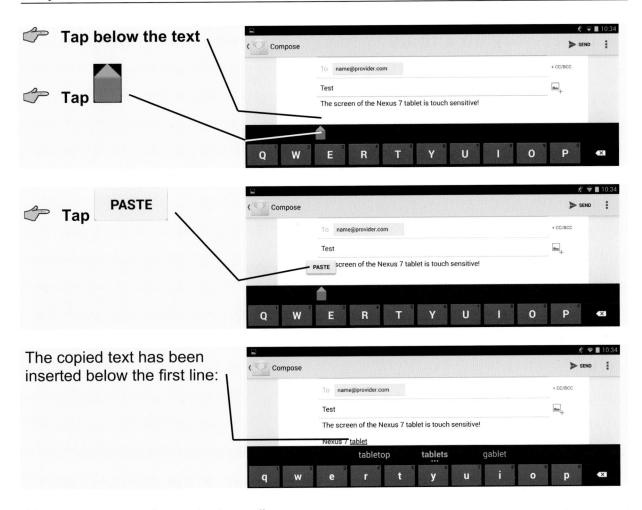

Tap PASTE

The copied text has been inserted below the first line:

Now you can send your test email:

Tap SEND

When your email message has been sent, and if the tablet's sound is turned on, you will hear a sound signal.

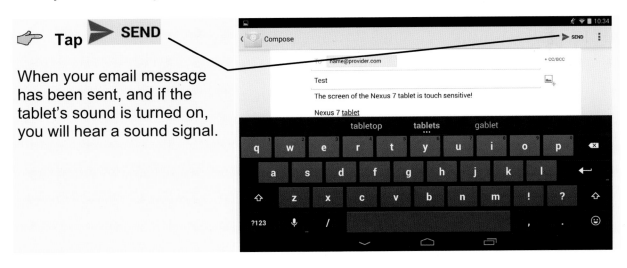

2.3 Receiving an Email Message

Once you have sent your message, the message will be received shortly afterwards. It will appear in your *Inbox*.

To open the *Inbox*:

☞ **Tap**

The number indicates that there are unread messages:

☞ **Tap** Inbox

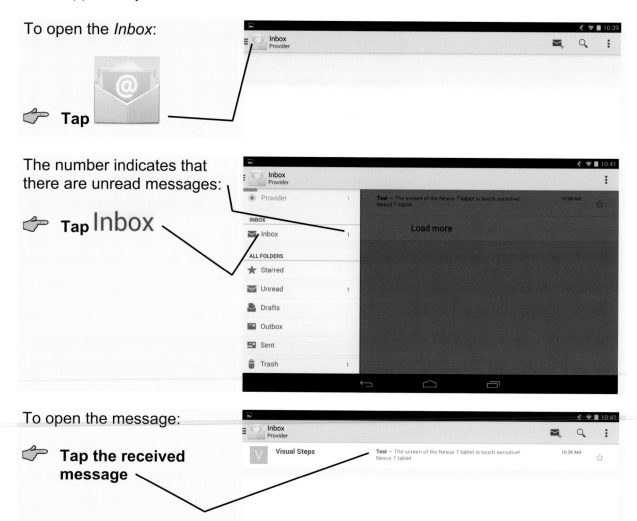

To open the message:

☞ **Tap the received message**

HELP! I do not receive any email.

If you do not receive the email right away, you can use the refresh option. At the top of the screen:

☞ **Tap**

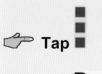

☞ Tap Refresh

You will see the content of the message:

The toolbar above the message contains a number of buttons. Here is what these buttons do:

Reply to a message.

Reply to all.

Forward a message.

Mark a message.

In the bar on the top right-hand side you will see even more buttons. This is what they do:

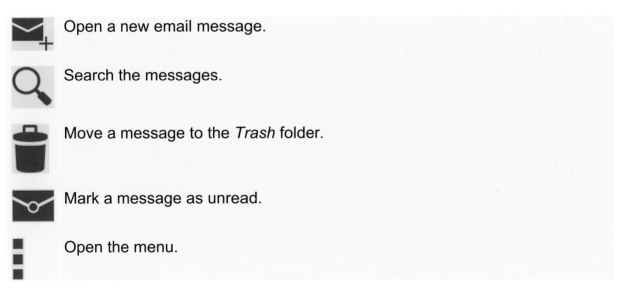

Open a new email message.

Search the messages.

Move a message to the *Trash* folder.

Mark a message as unread.

Open the menu.

This is how you display the
folder list again:

☞ **Tap**

2.4 Deleting an Email Message

You can delete your test message easily by simply swiping it off the screen:

☞ **Drag the message to**
the left side of the
screen

The email is deleted:

💡 **Tip**
Delete message
You can also delete a message like this:

☞ **Tap the message**

☞ **Tap** 🗑

The email has been moved to the *Trash* folder. You can verify this:

👉 **Tap**

👉 **Tap** 🗑 Trash

The deleted message has been placed in the *Trash* folder: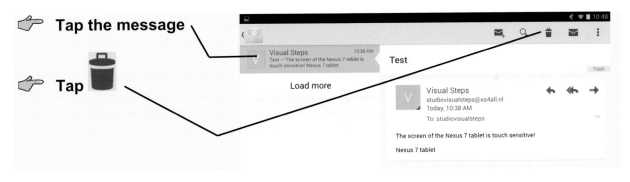

If you want, you can permanently delete the email message from the *Trash* folder:

👉 **Tap the message**

👉 **Tap** 🗑

👉 **Go back to the Home screen** 👣²

👉 **Lock the tablet, if you wish, or turn it off** 👣⁵

In this chapter you have learned how to use the *Email* app on the Google Nexus tablet to send, receive, and delete email messages.

2.5 Background Information

Dictionary

Account	A combination of a username and a password, which provides access to a specific, private service. A subscription with an Internet service provider is also called an account.
Email	A standard app that lets you send and receive email messages to and from various providers.
Gmail	A free web-based email service offered by the manufacturers of the well-known *Google Search* engine. The app with which you send and receive *Gmail* messages is also called *Gmail*.
Inbox	A folder where you can receive and view your email messages.
People	A standard app with which you can view and edit the information about your contacts.
Signature	A standard salutation that is inserted at the bottom of all your outgoing email messages.
Trash	A folder in which the deleted messages are stored. Once you delete a message from the *Trash* it will be deleted permanently.
Word Prediction	A function that displays suggestions for the word you are typing, while you are typing it.

Source: Google Nexus tablet and Gmail User Guide

2.6 Tips

 Tip

Add a signature to the messages you send
You can insert a standard text at the bottom of each email you send. For instance, a standard salutation for all your messages, or your name and address. This text is called your *signature*. This is how you add a signature:

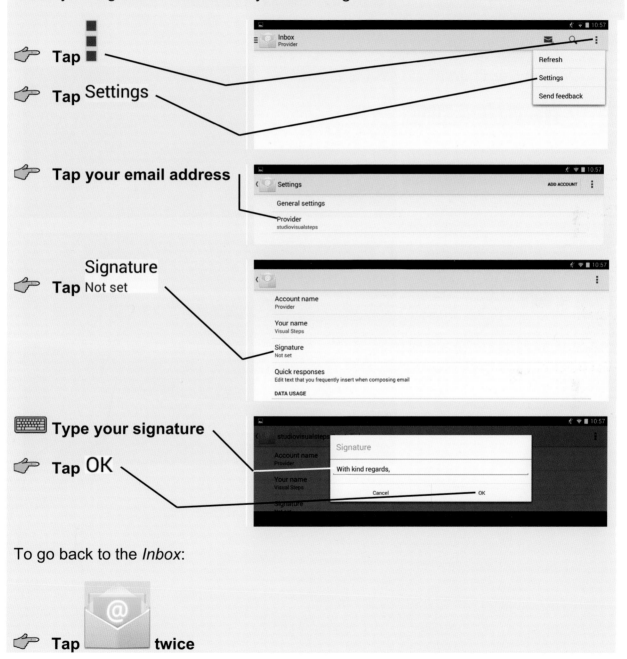

☞ **Tap** ▪

☞ **Tap** Settings

☞ **Tap your email address**

☞ **Tap** Signature Not set

⌨ **Type your signature**

☞ **Tap** OK

To go back to the *Inbox*:

☞ **Tap** @ **twice**

Tip

Disable Word Prediction

The *Word Prediction* function on the Google Nexus tablet may lead to unwanted corrections. The dictionary will not recognize every word you type but will keep trying to suggest alternative words. This can result in strange corrections, especially if you have made some spelling errors and did not notice these. Without knowing it, you may have accepted these corrections by typing a period, a comma, or a blank space. This is how you disable the *Word Prediction* function:

☞ **Open the *Settings* screen** ✂³

👉 **Drag upwards until you see**
 [A] Language & input

👉 **Tap**
 [A] Language & input

👉 **By**
 Google Keyboard,
 tap ⚏

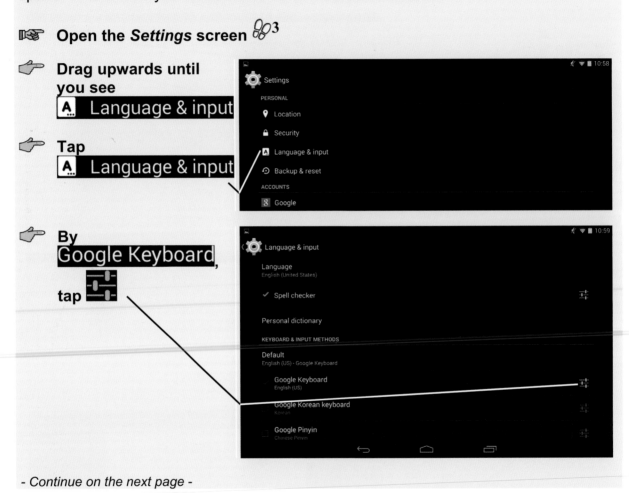

- Continue on the next page -

You will see various keyboard settings:

👉 **Drag upwards until you see**
Show correction sugges

👉 **Tap**
Show correction sugges

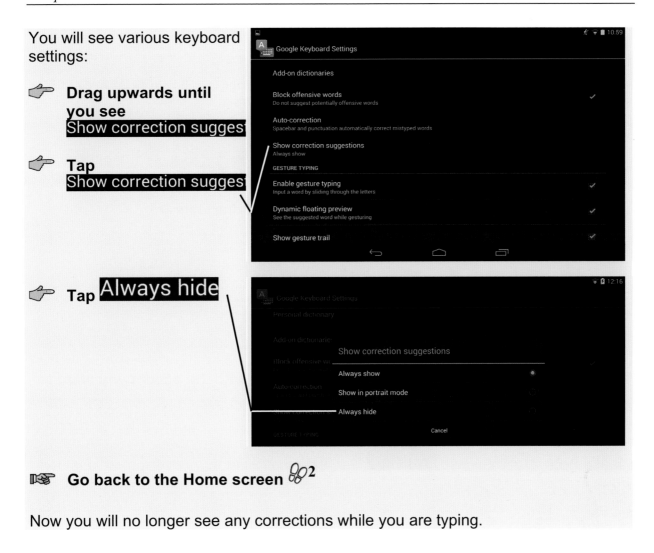

👉 **Tap Always hide**

👉 **Go back to the Home screen** 👣**2**

Now you will no longer see any corrections while you are typing.

💡 Tip

Typing foreign language characters

Onscreen keyboards do not have any letters that contain accent marks. But you can still type these letters and other special characters as well:

☞ **For example, press your finger on the** [e³] **key**

You will see a small window with a variety of options for the letter "e"

ē ê ë

é 3 è

☞ **Slide your finger from** [e] **to the letter e with the accent you want to use**

Please note: if you release [e] first, the small window will disappear. Just try it again.

☞ **Release the key**

The accented e will be inserted into the text.

3. Surfing with Your Tablet

In this chapter you will become acquainted with the *Chrome* app. This is the web browser application on your Google Nexus tablet. You can use this app to surf the Internet on your tablet. If you have used your computer to surf the Internet, you will see that surfing the Internet with your tablet is just as easy. The main difference is that you do not need a mouse. You surf the net by using touch gestures on the screen of your tablet.

You will learn how to open a web page on your tablet and will practice using a number of new touch gestures to zoom in, zoom out, and scroll. We explain how to open links (hyperlinks), switch back and forth between the pages you have opened and how to save bookmarks. You will also get acquainted with the search function in *Chrome*.

While you are surfing you may want to adjust certain settings. Since your tablet can handle multiple tasks at once, this will not be any problem. You can switch easily from one app to another. So let's get started!

In this chapter you will learn how to:

- open the *Chrome* app;
- open a web page;
- zoom in and zoom out;
- scroll;
- open a link on a web page;
- open a link in a new tab;
- add a bookmark;
- search;
- switch between recently used apps.

3.1 Opening the Chrome App

This is how you open the *Chrome* app, with which you can surf the Internet:

☞ **Unlock or turn on the tablet** 👣¹

You can open the *Chrome* app from the Home screen:

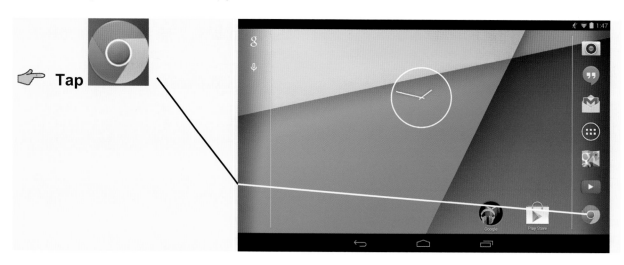

👉 **Tap**

🩹 HELP! The app is not displayed on the Home screen.

If the *Chrome* is not visible on your Home screen, you can open it like this:

👉 **Tap**

You may see this window:

👉 **If necessary, tap**
No thanks

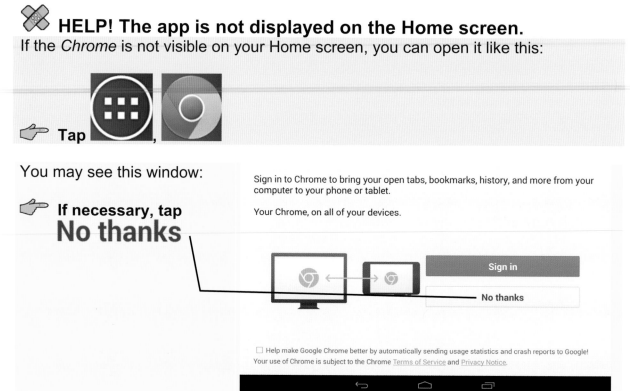

Sign in to Chrome to bring your open tabs, bookmarks, history, and more from your computer to your phone or tablet.

Your Chrome, on all of your devices.

Sign in

No thanks

☐ Help make Google Chrome better by automatically sending usage statistics and crash reports to Google! Your use of Chrome is subject to the Chrome Terms of Service and Privacy Notice.

You will see one or two tabs and a blank page:

Please note: you may also see other pages.

In this example you will see two tabs. You can close one of these tabs:

👉 **If necessary, tap** ✕

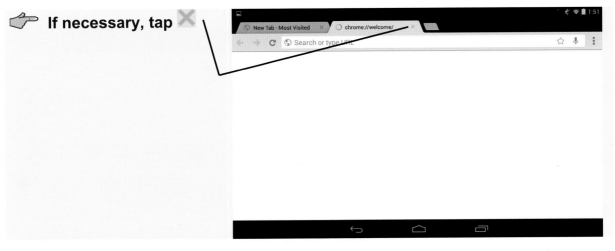

You will see the most visited page:

Please note: you may see a link to different page than the one shown here.

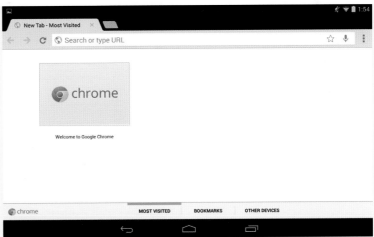

3.2 Opening a Web Page

In order to type a web address you need to display the onscreen keyboard:

☞ **Tap the address bar**

The onscreen keyboard will appear at the bottom of the screen:

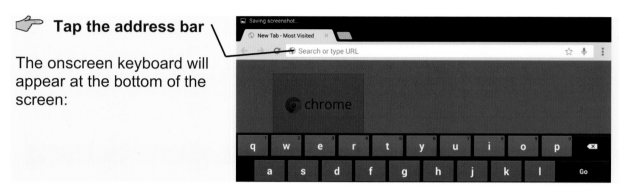

You can practice opening a page by taking a glimpse of the Visual Steps website:

⌨ **Type:** www.

Almost immediately, you will see a few suggestions:

The more letters of the web address you type, the more specific the suggestions will become.

⌨ **Type:**
visualsteps.com

After you have finished typing:

☞ **Tap** **Go**

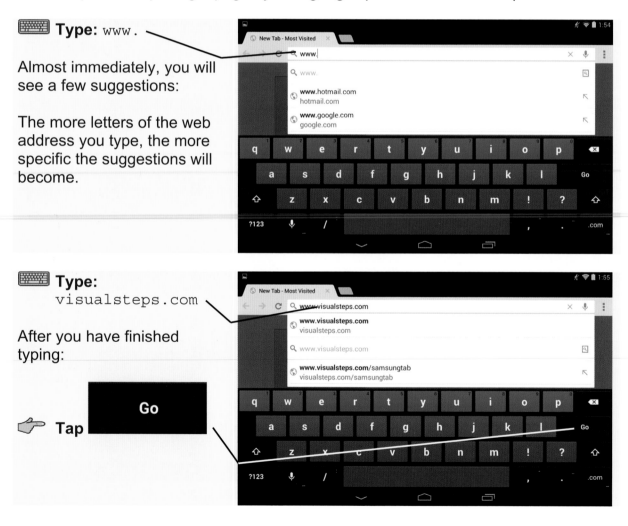

Tip

Use a suggestion

www.visualsteps.com

You can also tap visualsteps.com at once from the list of suggestions.

Here you see the Visual
Steps website:

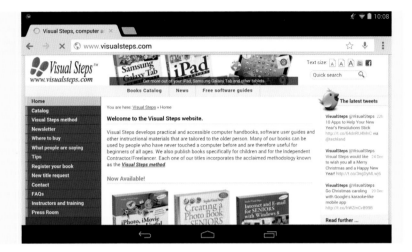

3.3 Zooming In and Out

If you think the letters and images on a website are too small, you can zoom in. You
do this by double-tapping. This means you tap the desired spot twice in rapid
succession:

☞ **Double-tap the menu
on the left-hand side**

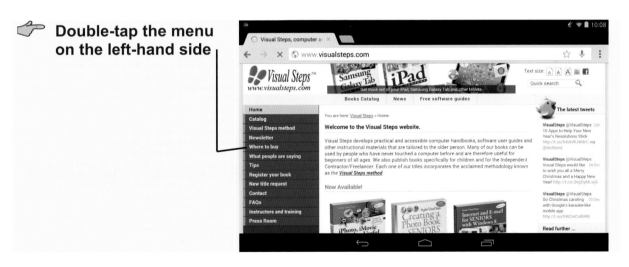

HELP! A different web page is opened.

If the double-tapping is not done correctly, you may have opened a different web page by mistake. In that case, just tap ⬅ in the top left-hand corner of the screen and try again. You can also practice double-tapping in a blank area of the screen.

Here you see that the web page has been enlarged:

☞ **Double-tap the menu once again**

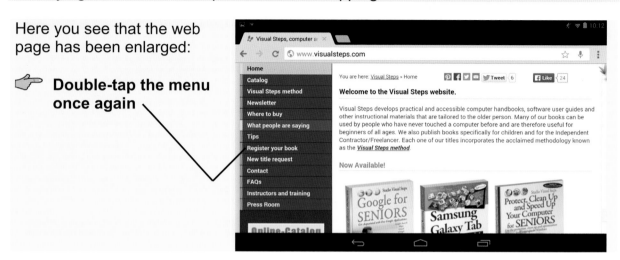

Now you have zoomed out to the normal view again. There is also another way to zoom in and out. You use two fingers to do this:

☞ **Move your thumb and index finger towards each other while touching the screen**

(pinch in)

You will see that everything becomes smaller.

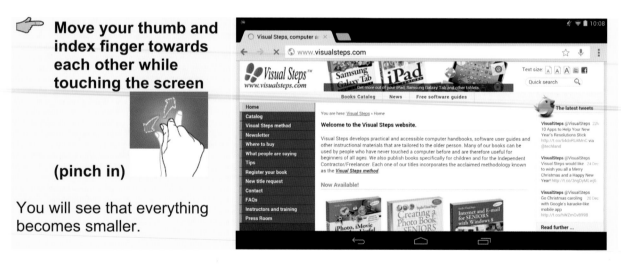

You can zoom in again by making the gesture in reverse:

 Spread your thumb and index finger away from each other while touching the screen

(pinch out)

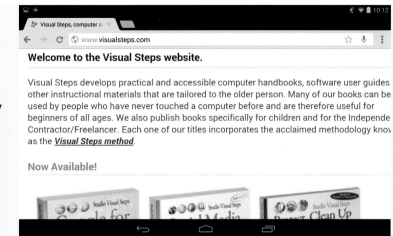

To go back to the normal view:

 Double-tap the page

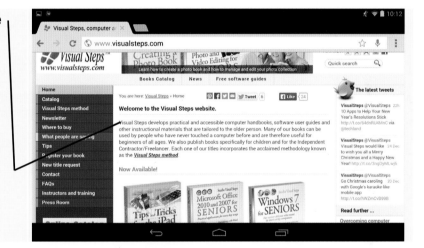

You will see the normal view again:

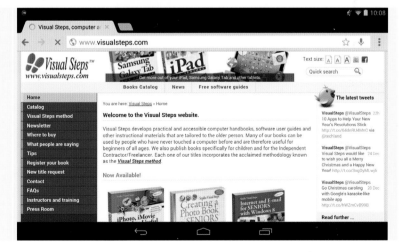

3.4 Scrolling

Scrolling allows you to view the content of a web page that is off screen. You can slide a web page up or down, or to the right or left. On your tablet you use your fingers to scroll through a web page:

 Drag your finger gently upwards over the screen

You will notice that you are scrolling downwards on the page:

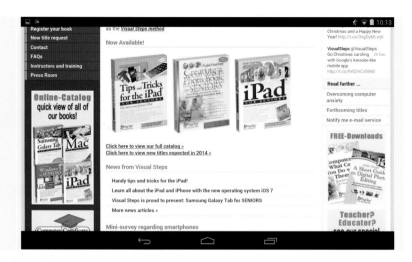

 Drag your finger gently downwards over the screen

Now you will be scrolling upwards on the page:

 Tip

Scrolling sideways
On a larger and broader web page you can scroll sideways by moving your finger horizontally across the screen from right to left or from left to right.

If you want to quickly scroll through a page you can use a swiping or flicking gesture:

 Swipe or flick the screen upwards

You can see the page moving quickly towards the bottom of the content:

 Tip

Move in different directions
By swiping the screen in the opposite direction (flicking downwards) you will get to the top of the page again. You can also move quickly to the right or left by swiping horizontally.

This is how you get to the top of the page:

 Swipe or flick the screen downwards

You will see the top of the web page again:

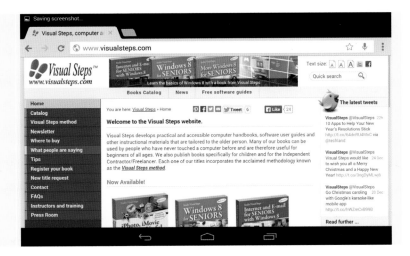

3.5 Opening a Link On a Web Page

If a page contains a link (also called a hyperlink) you can open it by tapping it. Just give it a try:

 Tap

 **HELP! I cannot tap the link.**
If you find it difficult to tap the correct link, you can zoom in first. The links will be displayed a bit larger and tapping a link will become easier.

☞ **If necessary, tap**

Here you see the Where to find our products web page from Visual Steps:

3.6 Opening a Link On a New Tab

You can also open a link in a new tab:

☞ **Press your finger on**
Catalog

After a moment, a menu will appear:

☞ **Tap** Open in new tab

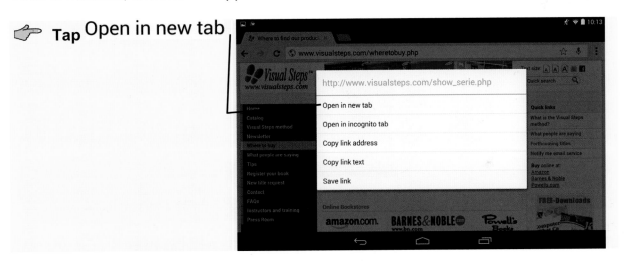

The linked page will be opened in a new tab. This is how you go to that tab:

☞ **Tap**
The Visual Steps Cat

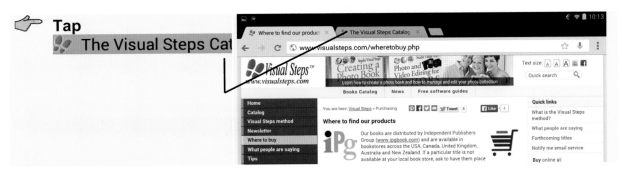

You will see the page with the
Visual Steps catalog:

This is how you close an open tab:

☞ **Tap**

You will see the Where to find
our products web page once
more:

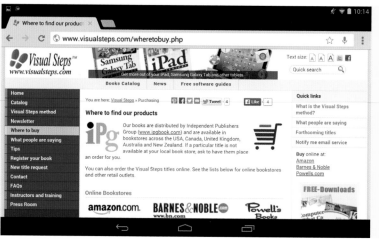

You can also open a new, blank tab just as easily:

☞ **Tap**

You will see the new tab:

3.7 Adding a Bookmark

If you want to visit a certain page regularly you can add a *bookmark* for this page. A bookmark refers to a website you want to save and visit again later on. By setting a bookmark for a page, you can go to the page very quickly without having to fill in the web address each time. This is how you add a bookmark:

☞ **Tap the first tab**

☞ Tap **Home**

☞ Tap ☆

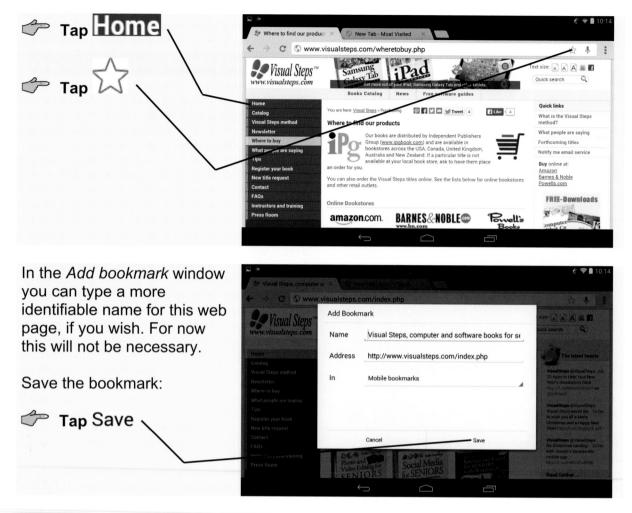

In the *Add bookmark* window you can type a more identifiable name for this web page, if you wish. For now this will not be necessary.

Save the bookmark:

☞ **Tap Save**

The web page has been added to your bookmarks. You can check to make sure:

☞ **Tap the second tab**

☞ **Tap** ▪

☞ **Tap Bookmarks**

You will see this screen:

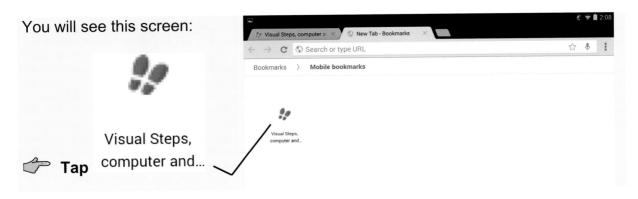

☞ **Tap**   Visual Steps, computer and...

You will see the Visual Steps website again.

3.8 Searching

In *Chrome* the address bar can be used as a search box. Just type your keywords directly into the address bar and see what happens:

☞ **Tap the address bar**

⌨ **Type:** Nexus 7 tablet sleeve

While you are typing you will see all sorts of suggestions for your keywords. You can use a suggestion by tapping it. For now this will not be necessary.

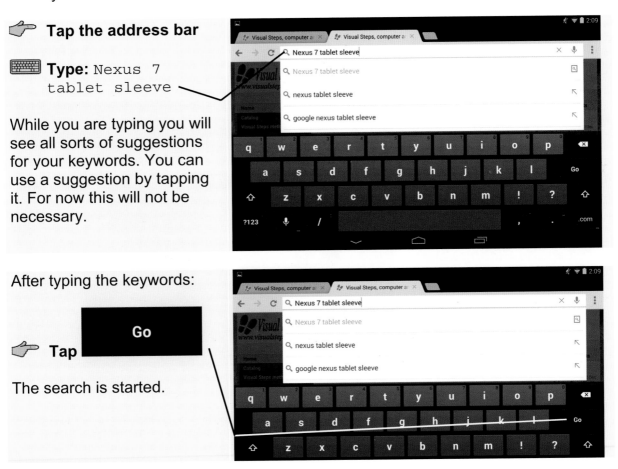

After typing the keywords:

☞ **Tap** Go

The search is started.

You will see the search results:

Tap a link to view a result. For now this will not be necessary.

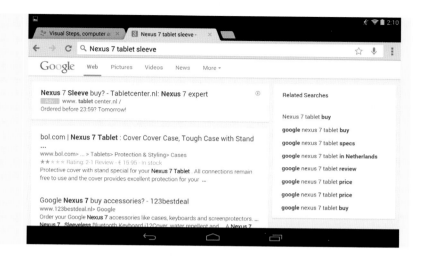

3.9 Switching Between Recently Used Apps

By tapping a button on the system bar you can switch between the apps you have recently used. Just try it:

 At the bottom of the screen, tap

You will see a menu with recently used apps:

In this example you see four apps. On your own tablet other apps may be shown as well.

 Tap the *Settings* app for example

You will see the *Settings* screen:

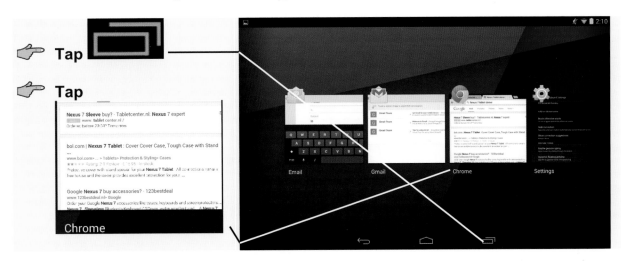

Now you see the *Chrome* screen again.

👉 **Go back to the Home screen** 👣²

👉 **Lock or turn off the tablet, if you wish** 👣⁵

3.10 Background Information

Dictionary

Bookmark	A link to a web address saved in a list. Bookmarks allow you to go to web pages quickly without the need of any typing.
Chrome	An app on your tablet that allows you to surf the Internet.
Google	*Google* is mainly known for its search engine. But the company also provides other services, such as *Google Maps* (for directions and trips), *Chrome* and *Hangouts* (an app that lets you chat with others).
Link, hyperlink	A link is a navigational tool on a web page that automatically leads the user to the relevant information when tapped. A link may take the shape of a text message or an image, such as a picture, a button or an icon. Also called a hyperlink.
Scrolling	Allowing a web page to move across the screen; this can be done upwards, downwards, to the left, or to the right. On the Google Nexus tablet you use touch gestures to do this.
Zoom in	Take a closer look at an item; the letters and images will become larger.
Zoom out	View an item from a distance, the letters and images will become smaller.

Source: Nexus 7 Tablet User Guide, Wikipedia

3.11 Tips

Tip
Clear history

In the history, all recently visited websites are stored. This helps to load web pages quicker the next time you visit the website. You can also delete this browser history, if you want:

Tap

Tap History

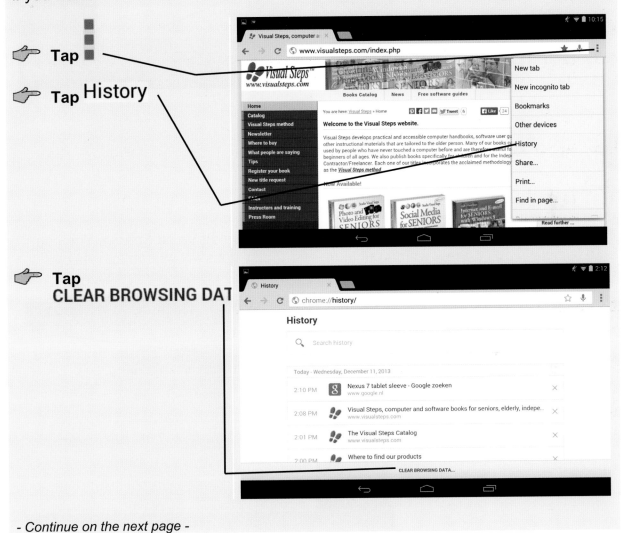

Tap
CLEAR BROWSING DAT

- Continue on the next page -

If you want, you can select
desired components:

☞ **Tap** Clear

The browser history will be
deleted.

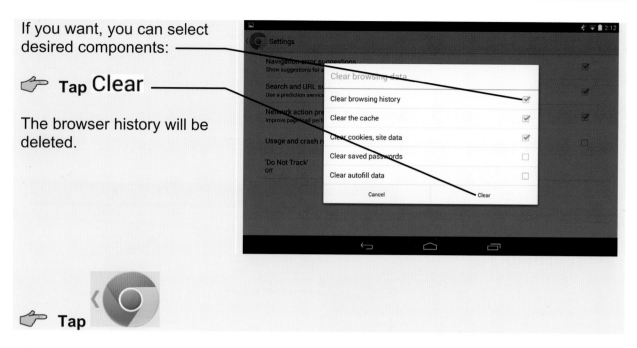

☞ **Tap**

💡 **Tip**

Voice search
The Google Nexus tablet is equipped with a function called *Voice Search*. You can
say a single word or a few words out loud, and the system will search for relevant
web pages.

☞ **In the address bar, tap**

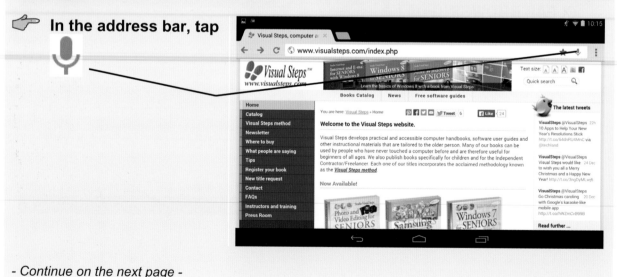

- Continue on the next page -

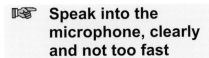 **Speak into the microphone, clearly and not too fast**

You will see the search results:

 **Tap a suggestion, if you wish**

Or:

 **Tap** Go

Keep in mind that *Chrome* will not always find the correct results.

💡 **Tip**

Google Search
On the Home screen you can open the *Google Search* app by tapping g :

On the Google Nexus 10, tap Google.

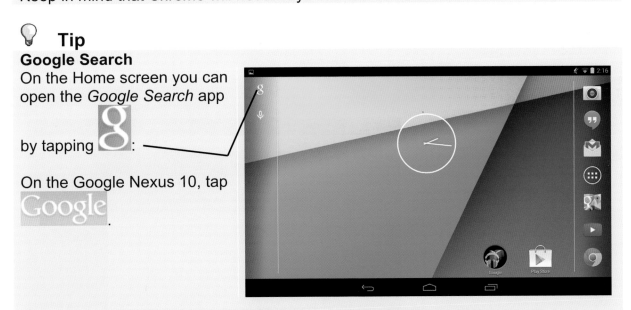

You will eventually end up in the *Chrome* app as well. The first time you open *Google Search* you will see a couple of screens regarding *Google Now*. You can find more information about *Google Now* in the tips at the end of *Chapter 4 The Standard Apps On Your Google Nexus Tablet*.

☀ Tip

Delete a bookmark

If you no longer want to use a bookmark, you can delete it like this:

☞ Tap ⋮

☞ Tap Bookmarks

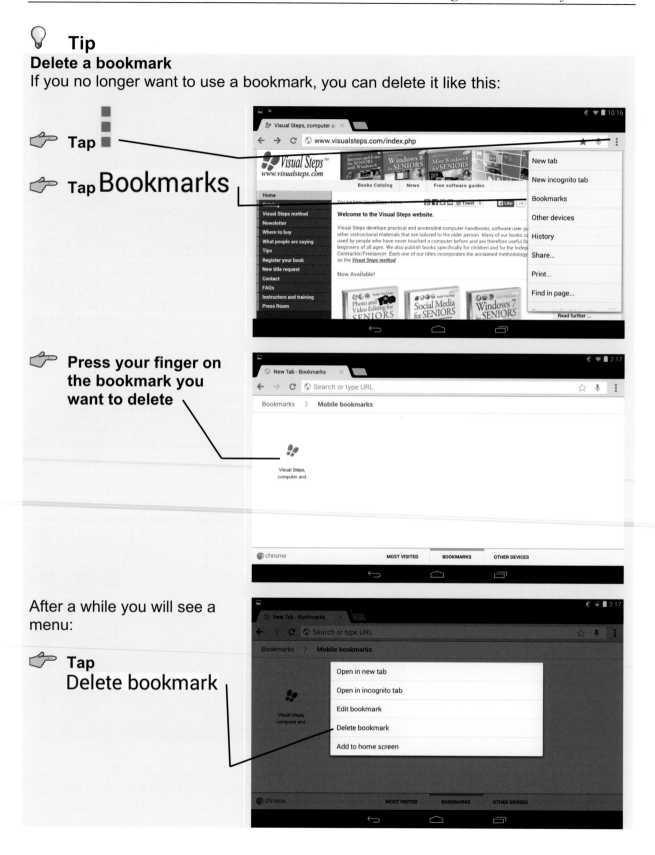

☞ Press your finger on the bookmark you want to delete

After a while you will see a menu:

☞ Tap Delete bookmark

4. The Standard Apps on Your Google Nexus Tablet

Along with *Email* and *Chrome*, you will find other useful apps already installed on your Google Nexus tablet. The *People* app for instance, allows you to add and edit information about your contacts. You can jot down appointments and keep track of events with the *Calendar* app.

You can use the *Maps* app to look up an address or well-known location. Then you can view the location on a regular map or on a satellite photo. Many locations also have an option to open *Google Street View*. This function makes it look as if you are standing there yourself. Once you have found the desired location you can get directions on how to get there.

Google Search is the search function of your Google Nexus tablet. You can search your apps, contacts, messages, and music stored on your tablet and if you are connected to the Internet you can use *Google Search* to search the Internet.

In this chapter you will learn how to:

- add contacts in the *People* app;
- edit and delete contacts;
- add an event in the *Calendar* app;
- determine your current location in the *Maps* app;
- use layers for viewing the screen;
- find a location and get directions;
- search with the *Google Search* app;
- closing apps.

4.1 Adding Contacts

You can open the *People* app from the apps overview screen:

☞ **Unlock or turn on your tablet** 𝜚𝜚¹

☞ **Tap**

☞ **Tap** People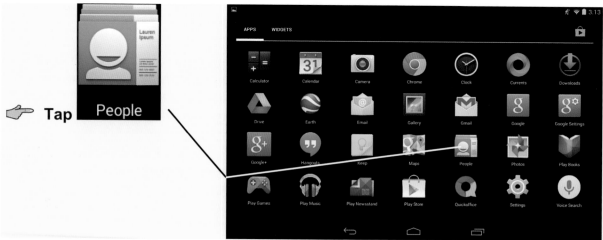

In this example you will see
the *Google* account that is
linked to this tablet:

☞ **Tap**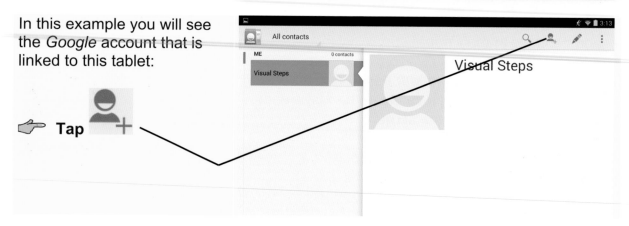

💡 **Tip**

Contacts from your Google account
If you have added contacts to your *Google* account on another device, such as a
mobile phone, they will also be displayed (synchronized) automatically on your
Google Nexus tablet if you are connected to the Internet.

☞ **Tap** OK

> Your new contact will be synchronized with vsteps8@gmail.com.
>
> Add new account　　　　　　　　　　　OK

You will see the window in which you can add a new contact:

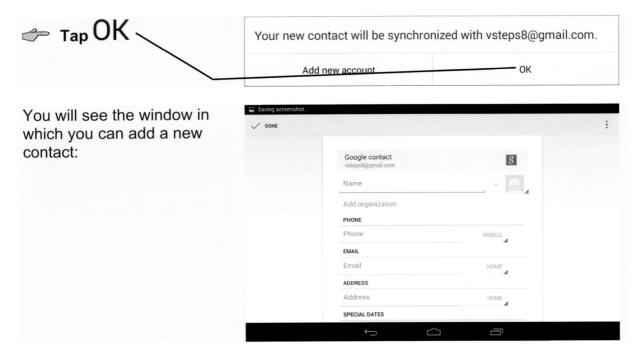

In this example we will add a fictitious new contact using the onscreen keyboard. You can enter the information about someone you really know, if you like:

⌨ **Type the first and last name of your contact**

☞ **Drag upwards until you see** Phone

☞ **Tap** Phone

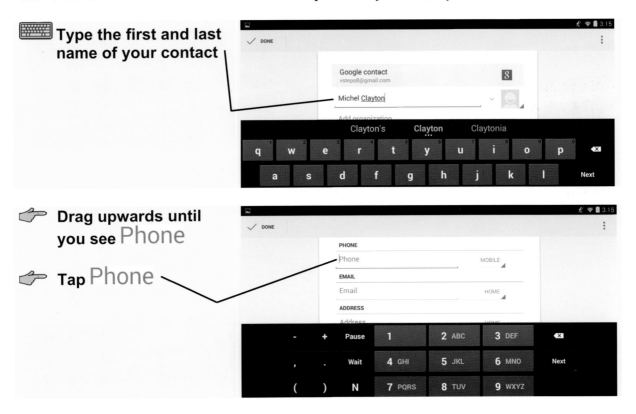

In this field you can enter the mobile (cell) phone number:

 Type your contact's mobile phone number

Add a new line for yet another phone number:

☞ **Tap** Add new

↘ **Please note:**

When you type a phone number, the blank spaces will be filled in automatically.

The default label for the next phone number is ___WORK___◢. You can change this label and turn it into a private phone number:

☞ **Tap** WORK ___◢

You will see a list of labels you can choose from:

☞ **Tap** HOME

Type your contact's home phone number

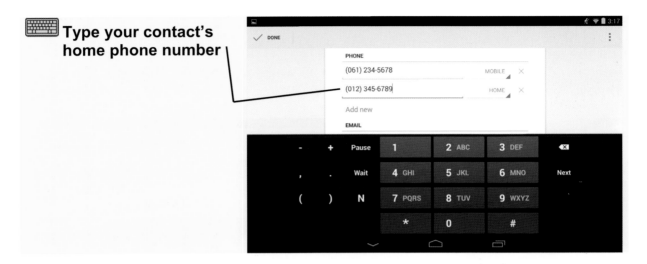

Now enter the email address. If you want, you can also enter the home address or other information:

Drag upwards until you see Email and Address

Tap Email

Type your contact's email address

Tap Address

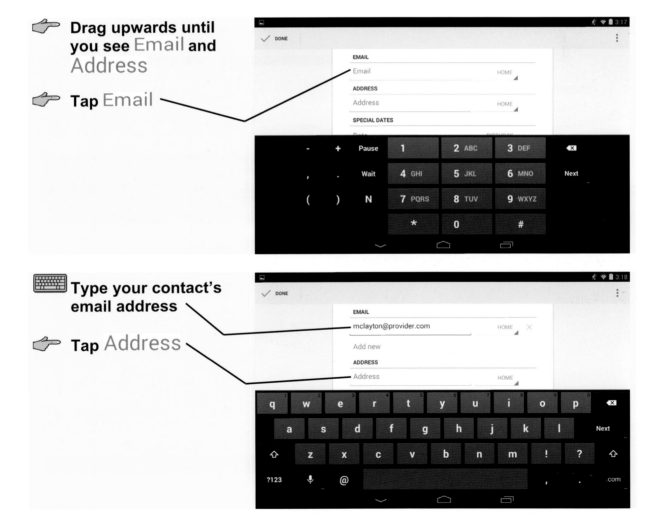

Tip

Edit the label
You can edit the label for the email address as well; for example, change it from home to work.

Type the street name and home number

If you want to go to the next line, simply:

☞ **Tap**

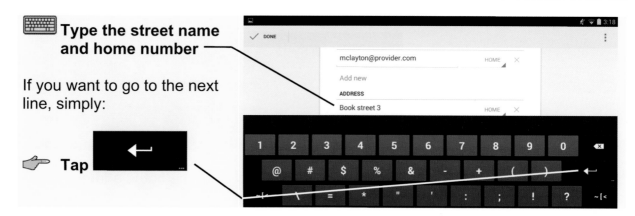

Add the postal/zip code and the city:

Type the postal/zip code and the name of the city

Save the contact:

☞ **Tap** ✓ **DONE**

Now your contact has been added to the list:

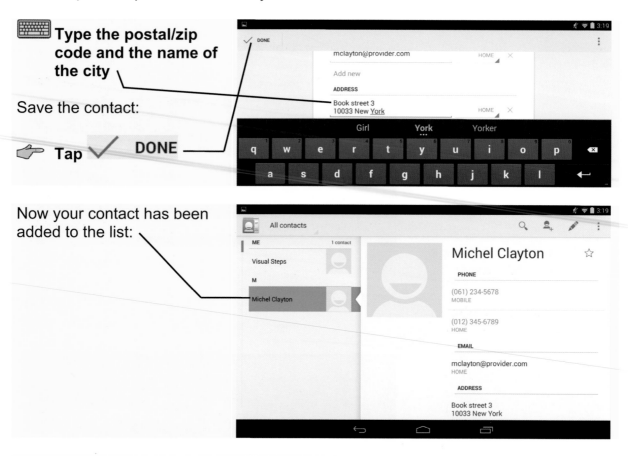

☞ **Add three more contacts** ℘7

4.2 Editing a Contact

After you have added all your contacts you may want to edit the information. For instance, if you want to change an address, add a second email address or a new phone number. This is how you open a contact in order to edit it:

Tap the desired contact

Tap

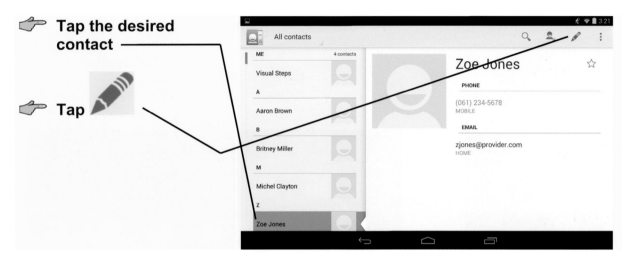

This is how you edit the phone number, for example:

If necessary, drag upwards until you see the phone number

Press your finger on the phone number

The phone number is selected:

You can type the new phone number right away:

Type the new phone number

Tap ✓ **DONE**

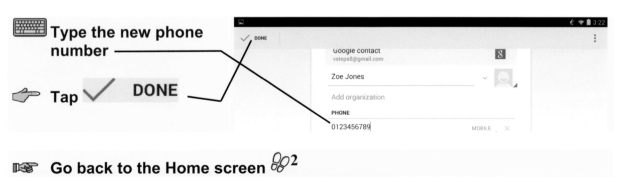

☞ **Go back to the Home screen** 👣²

In the *Tips* at the end of this chapter you will find tips on how to add, edit or delete fields, and how to delete a contact.

4.3 Calendar

In the *Calendar* app you can keep a calendar. This is how you open the app:

☞ **Tap**

☞ **Tap** Calendar

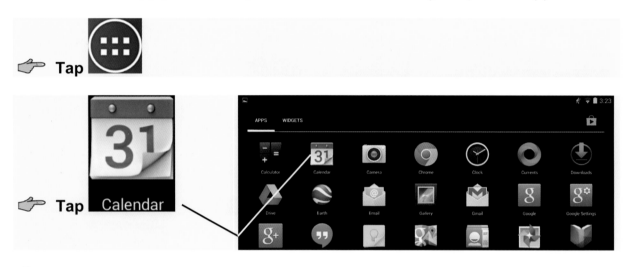

💡 **Tip**

Other events

If you have added events to your *Google* account on another device, such as a mobile phone, they will also be displayed (synchronized) automatically on your Google Nexus tablet if you are connected to the Internet.

The calendar will be opened with a view of the current week.

If you have selected a date other than today's date, you can tap the 11 **TODAY** button to quickly go back to the events of the current date:

If you have signed in with your tablet with multiple *Google* accounts, you can select which calendars you want to display:

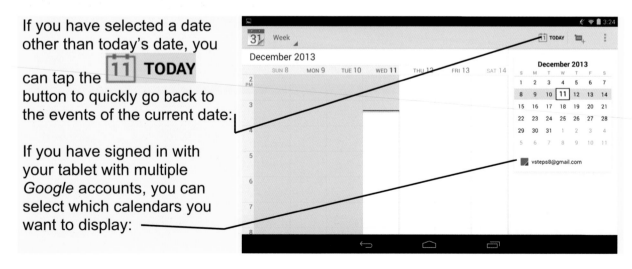

You can select a weekly, monthly, or yearly view. This is how to view a whole month:

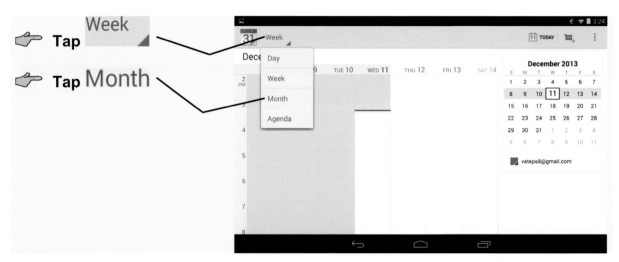

☞ **Tap** Week

☞ **Tap** Month

You will see a view of the current month:

This is how you quickly skip to the next month:

☞ **Swipe upwards until you see the next month**

The next month is displayed:

4.4 Adding Events

Here is how you add an event to your calendar.

☞ **Tap the desired day**

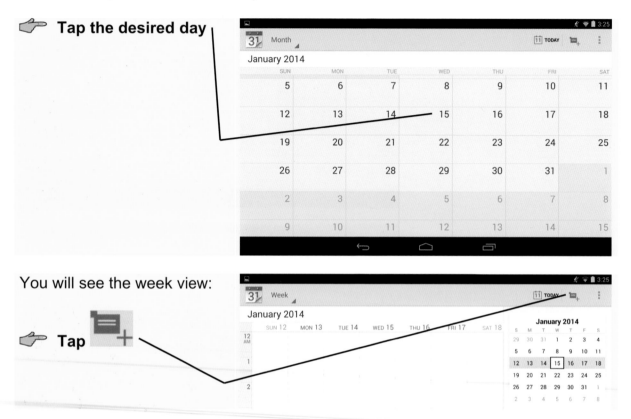

You will see the week view:

☞ **Tap** [icon]

Enter a name for the event:

⌨ **Type a name, for example:** Tennis lessons

Add a location too:

☞ **Tap** Location

Type a location, for example: Tennis court

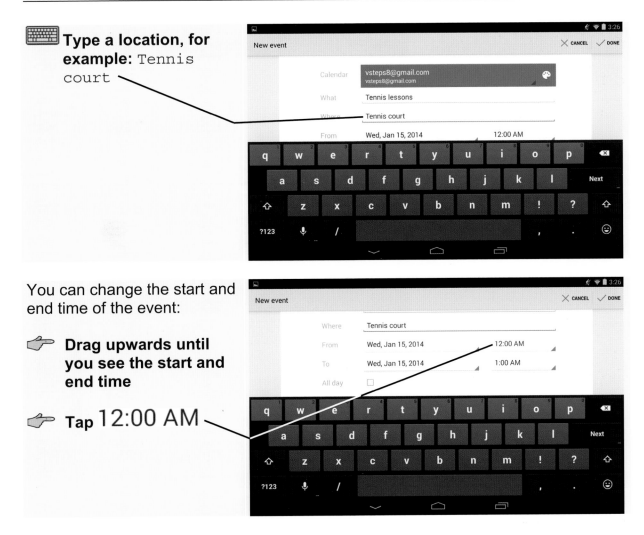

You can change the start and end time of the event:

☞ **Drag upwards until you see the start and end time**

☞ **Tap** 12:00 AM

You can change the hours and minutes:

☞ **Tap the desired hour**

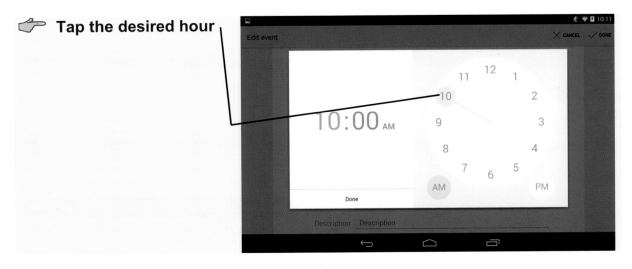

If you have tapped the hour, the minutes will be selected automatically:

☞ **Tap the desired number of minutes**

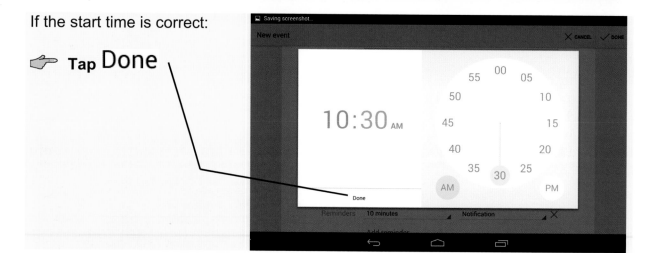

If the start time is correct:

☞ **Tap** Done

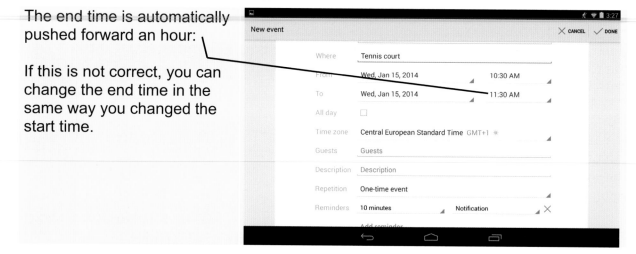

The end time is automatically pushed forward an hour:

If this is not correct, you can change the end time in the same way you changed the start time.

Tip

Correct start and end time
If you add an event by tapping a time box in the day view, the start and end time will be filled in automatically. You can always adjust these times.

 Tip

Whole day
If an event takes the entire day:

 Tap the checkmark ☑ **by** All day

You can use even more options in the window where you have added the event:

You can add the names of your guests, and a description of the event:

By Reminders you can set up the frequency in which the event needs to be repeated.

By default, the One-time event option has been selected:

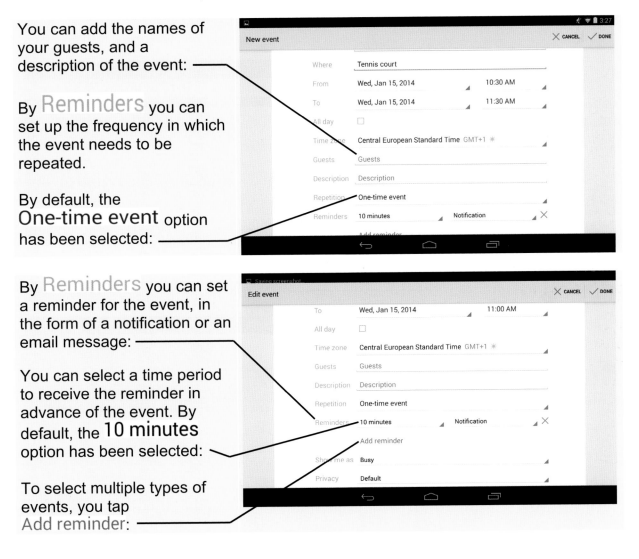

By Reminders you can set a reminder for the event, in the form of a notification or an email message:

You can select a time period to receive the reminder in advance of the event. By default, the 10 minutes option has been selected:

To select multiple types of events, you tap Add reminder:

The last two options only apply to a shared calendar. In the *Tips* at the end of this chapter you will find more information about sharing a calendar.

After you have entered all the information for this event:

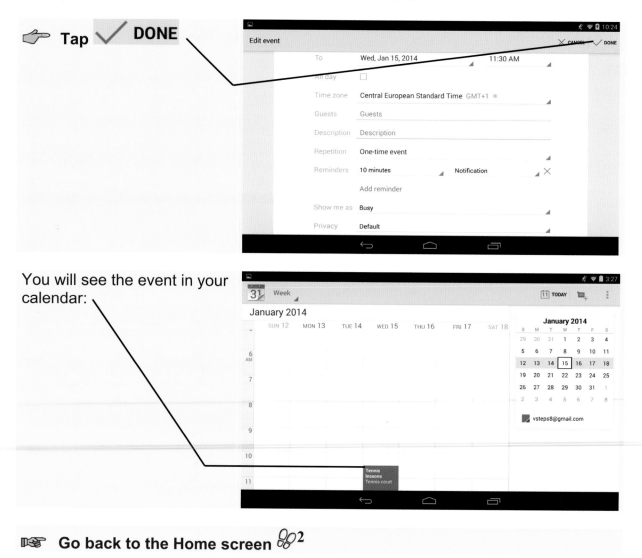

☞ Tap ✓ **DONE**

You will see the event in your calendar:

🖙 **Go back to the Home screen** 👣²

In the *Tips* at the end of this chapter you can read how to edit and delete an event.

4.5 Maps

With the *Maps* app you can search for a location and get directions. This is how you open the *Maps* app:

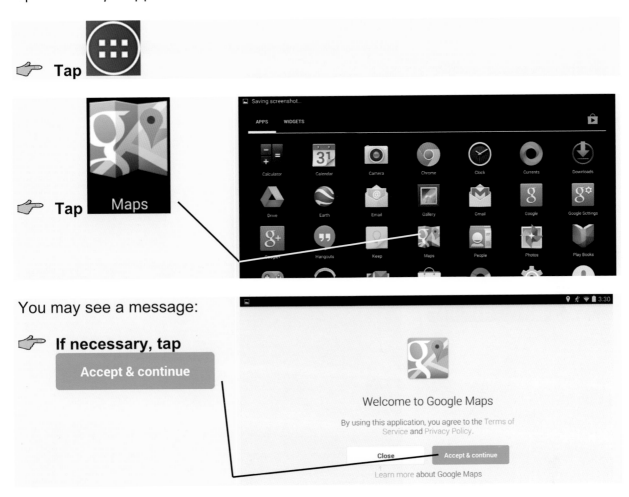

👉 **Tap**

👉 **Tap** Maps

You may see a message:

👉 **If necessary, tap**
Accept & continue

In the next screen:

👉 **If necessary, tap**
Yes, I'm in

HELP! I see a different screen.

If you see a different screen, you probably need to update your *Maps* app. You can read how to update an app in the *Tip Update apps* on page 164.

You will see a map:

Your map may look different than the one shown in this example.

You can change the view of the map by adding layers:

☞ **Tap**

☞ **Tap** Satellite

You will see a satellite photo:

 Tip

Zoom in and out

Move two fingers away from each other (spread) or towards each other (pinch) to zoom in or zoom out.

4.6 Finding a Location

In *Maps* you can search not only for addresses but also well-known public places:

The location has been found and is now marked with an

icon 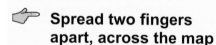:

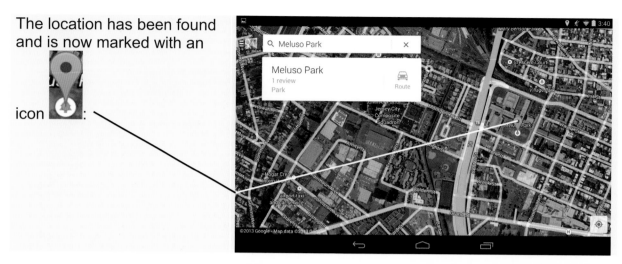

Zoom in on this location:

☞ **Spread two fingers apart, across the map**

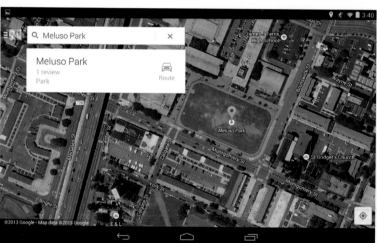

If you find a location that interests you, you can take an even closer look by using the *Street View* options in *Maps*:

☞ **Tap** Meluso Park

👉 **Tap the picture with Street View,**

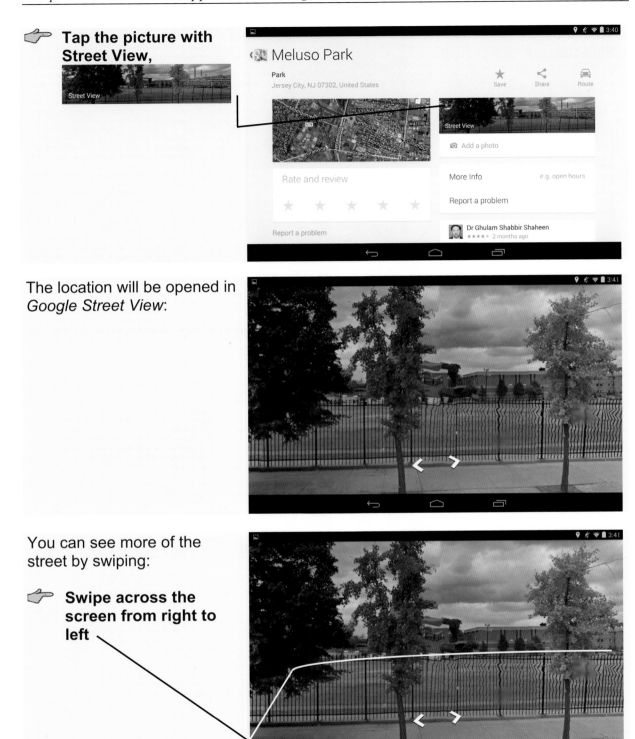

The location will be opened in *Google Street View*:

You can see more of the street by swiping:

👉 **Swipe across the screen from right to left**

More buildings and other objects will come into view:

To go back to the map view:

 Tap

 Tip

Extensive information

Many locations will offer extra information, such as an address or website:

You may also see reviews written by other visitors:

Here is an explanation of the various functions for the buttons in this screen:

 Save

Tap this icon to save the location as a favorite.

 Share

Tap this icon to share information about the location with others.

Route

Tap this icon to get directions.

4.7 Getting Directions

If you have found the desired location you can get directions on how to get there. You do that like this:

☞ **Tap**

☞ **Tap Route**

You can choose between traveling by car, public transport, bicycle or on foot:

You can reverse the starting and ending points, if desired.

You can practice by entering a starting point:

☞ **Tap** My Location

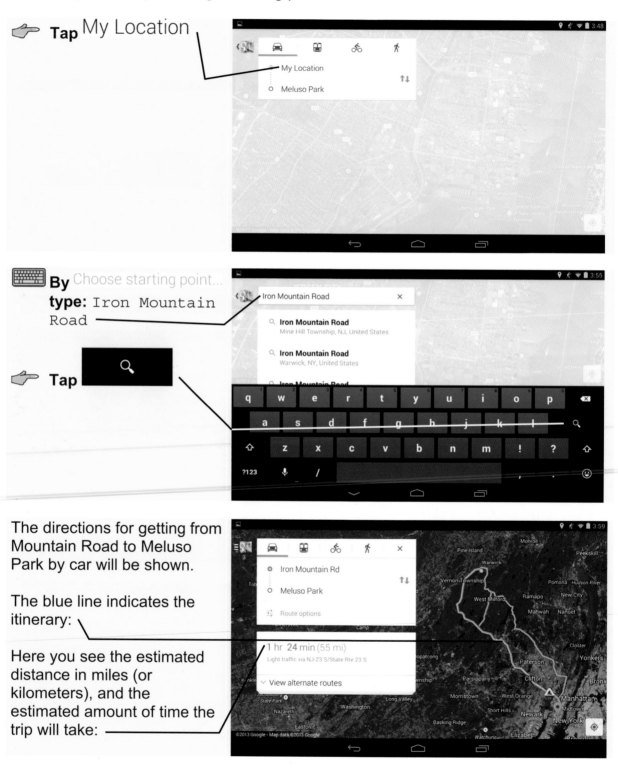

⌨ **By type:** Iron Mountain Road

☞ **Tap** 🔍

The directions for getting from Mountain Road to Meluso Park by car will be shown.

The blue line indicates the itinerary:

Here you see the estimated distance in miles (or kilometers), and the estimated amount of time the trip will take:

To open the directions:

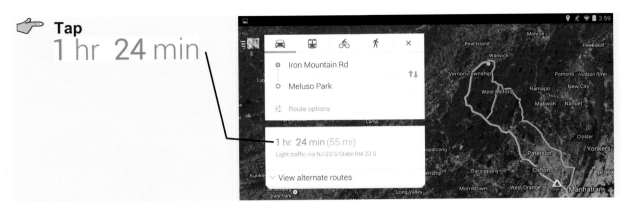

☞ **Tap**
1 hr 24 min

You will see the directions. By tapping the directions you can display a specific part of the itinerary:

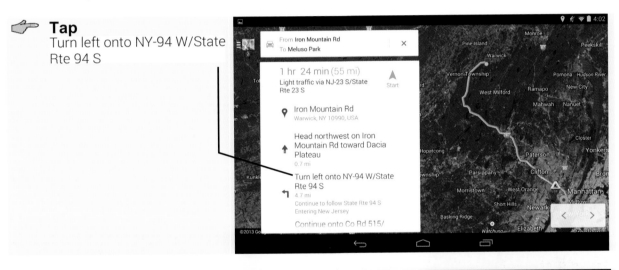

☞ **Tap**
Turn left onto NY-94 W/State Rte 94 S

You will see a smaller portion of the itinerary:

Now you can follow the itinerary step by step, by tapping the next instruction. For now you do not need to do this.

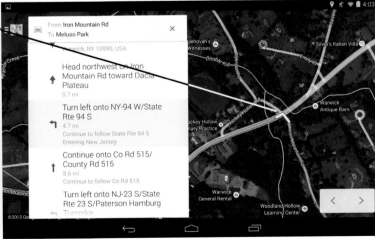

By zooming out you can display the full itinerary once more:

☞ **Drag the directions downwards**

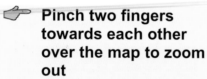

☞ **Tap** Start

You may see this window:

☞ **If necessary, tap** Cancel

Improve your location

Turn on the following to improve your location:
Network location

☐ Don't show again

| Cancel | Enable |

☞ **Pinch two fingers towards each other over the map to zoom out**

This makes the map smaller.

☞ **Repeat this step until you see the full route**

You can delete the route:

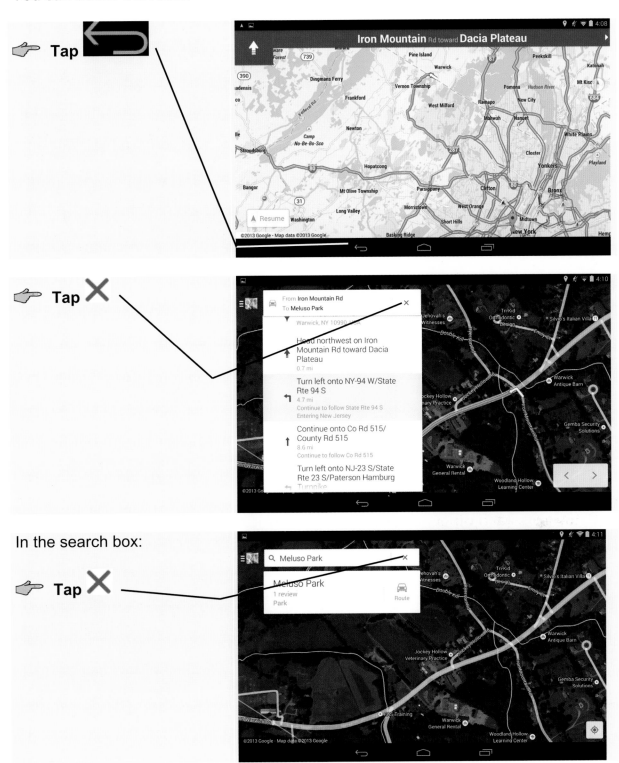

☞ **Tap**

☞ **Tap** ✕

In the search box:

☞ **Tap** ✕

The itinerary will be deleted. Now you can return to your current location:

☞ **Tap**

Here is your current location:

☞ **Go back to the Home screen** ∂∂²

4.8 Searching

The *Google Search* app is the standard search app on your tablet. You can use it to search your tablet's content and to search the Internet. This is how you open *Google Search*:

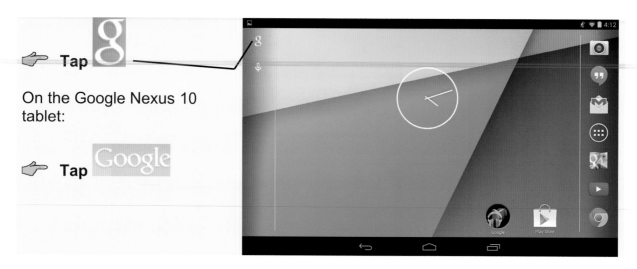

☞ **Tap**

On the Google Nexus 10 tablet:

☞ **Tap** Google

You may see information about *Google Now*:

☞ **If necessary, tap**

NEXT

In the next screen:

☞ **If necessary, tap**

YES, I'M IN.

The *Google Search* app will be opened. If Wi-Fi is not turned on, the app will only search the contents of your tablet. If Wi-Fi is turned on, the app will also search the Internet. In this example we will search the tablet for information about a specific contact:

☞ **Tap the search box**

⌨ **Type:** m

You will see the search results:

☞ **Drag the keyboard downwards**

In this example, a contact has been found as well:

☞ **Tap Michel Clayton**

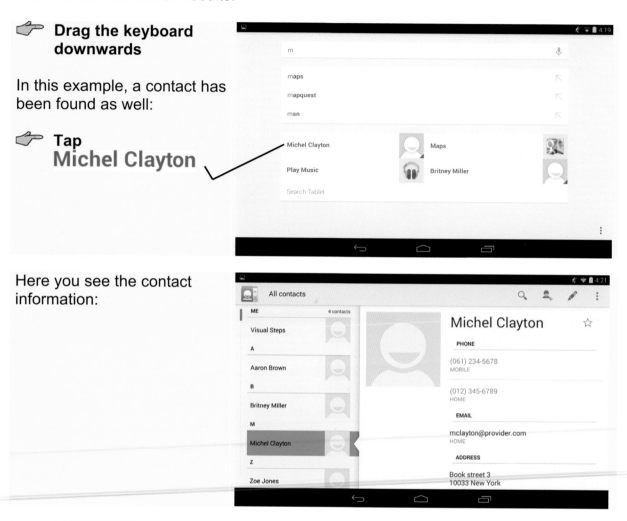

Here you see the contact information:

☞ **Go back to the Home screen** 🐾²

💡 Tip

App settings for Google Search

You can select the apps which *Google Search* is allowed to search:

☞ **Tap** ⋮

☞ **Tap Settings**

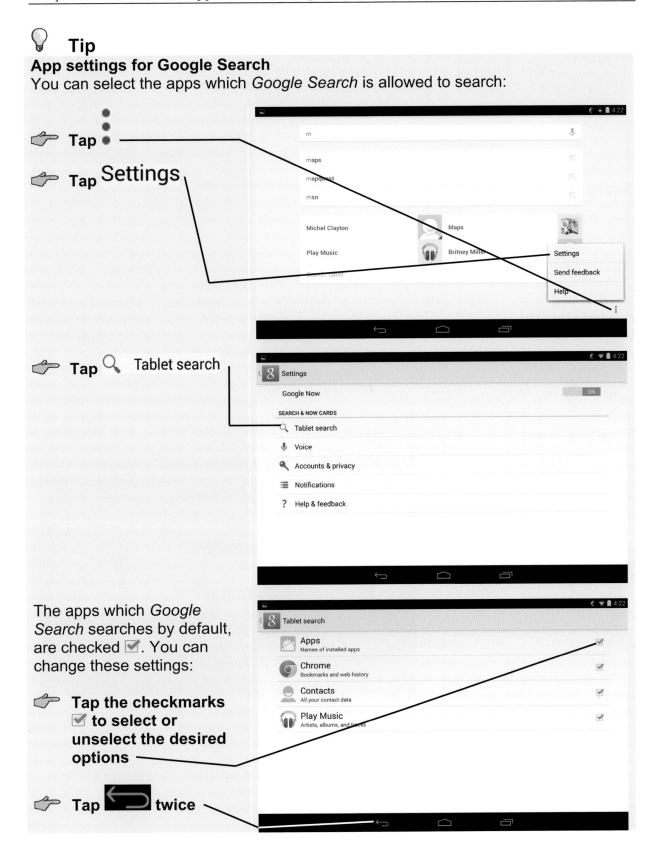

☞ **Tap** 🔍 **Tablet search**

The apps which *Google Search* searches by default, are checked ☑. You can change these settings:

☞ **Tap the checkmarks ☑ to select or unselect the desired options**

☞ **Tap ⬅ twice**

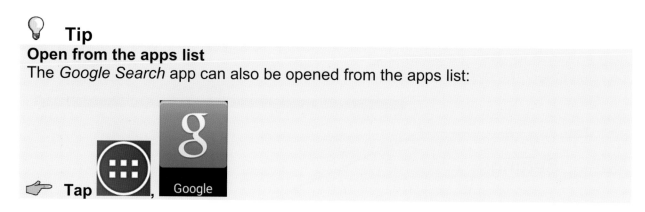

Tip
Open from the apps list
The *Google Search* app can also be opened from the apps list:

☞ **Tap** ⬤ , 🅖 Google

4.9 Closing Apps

By now you have worked with a number of different apps installed on your tablet. You have always returned to the Home screen after using such an app. Some of the apps will not turn off and will stay active in the background. This usually is not a problem, since your tablet does not use a lot of energy in sleep mode. There is also the advantage that apps respond quicker if they are already opened once you have unlocked your tablet.

Yet you can still close the apps you no longer use, if you want. You do that like this:

☞ **Tap** ▭

You will see the recently used apps:

☞ **Press your finger gently on the app you want to close**

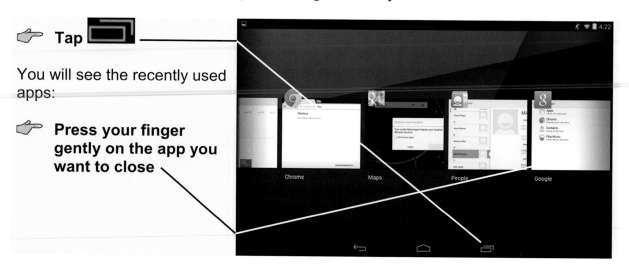

After a moment you will see a menu:

☞ **Tap**
Remove from list

The app is now closed.

☞ **Go back to the Home screen** %%²

☞ **Lock or turn off your tablet, if you wish** %%⁵

In this chapter you have learned to use various apps that are included in the standard package on your tablet. In the *Tips* at the end of this chapter you will find an overview and a brief description of the apps that have not been discussed at length in this book.

4.10 Background Information

Dictionary

Album	The name of a folder that contains pictures. These include the ones taken with your tablet, or those saved to your tablet by downloading them from an attachment or a website.
Field	An element where text can be entered such as information about a contact. *First name, Last name* and *Postal code* are some examples.
Google Calendar	*Google's* calendar application for keeping track of events and appointments. Requires a *Google* account in order to use it.
Google Maps	*Google's* map application. You can use it to find locations, look up addresses, get directions and view satellite photos.
Google Now	An extension of *Google Search*. *Google Now* provides extra information adapted to a specific user.
Google Search	The app that performs all searches on the Google Nexus tablet.
Label	The name of a field.
Outlook	An email program for use on a computer, part of the *Microsoft Office* suite.
People	An app in which you can add and manage your contacts.
Street View	One of the extra features in *Google Maps* with which you can view panoramic images at street level.
Synchronize	Matching data from your *Google* account automatically, so you see the same information on your computer and other mobile devices. Many apps allow you to enable or disable the synchronizing feature by adjusting the app's settings.
Windows Live Mail	An email program for use on a computer, part of *Windows Live Essentials*.

Source: Google Nexus Tablet User Guide, Wikipedia

4.11 Tips

Tip

Add a field
This is how you restore a deleted field or add an extra field in the *People* app:

☞ **Open the *People* app** 👣⁹

☞ **Tap the desired contact**

☞ **Tap** 🖊

☞ **Drag upwards until you see the desired field, for example, PHONE**

☞ **Tap Add new**

You can enter the data in the new field.

If you want to add a new field:

☞ **Drag all the way downwards**

☞ **Tap Add another field**

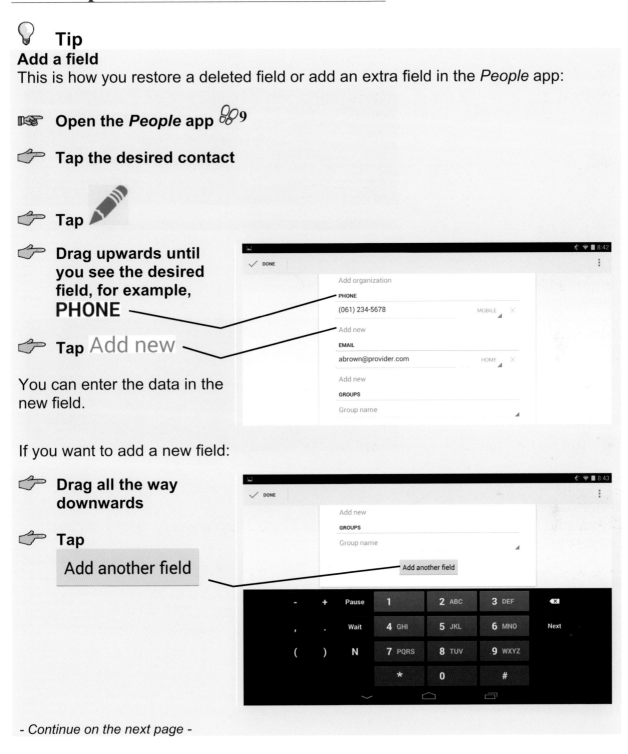

- Continue on the next page -

☞ **Tap a field, for example,**

Nickname

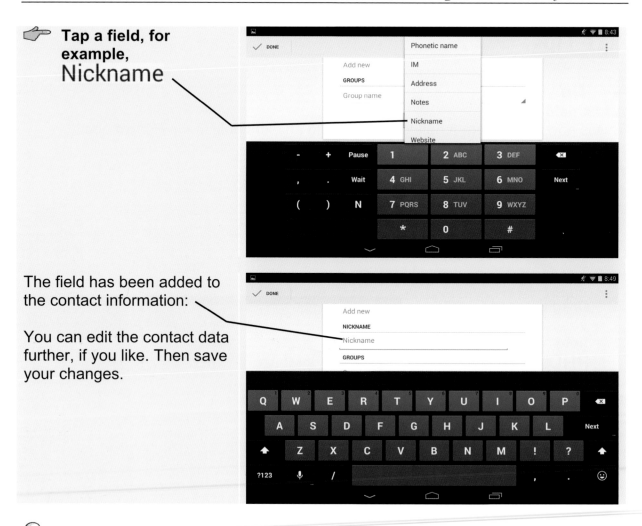

The field has been added to the contact information:

You can edit the contact data further, if you like. Then save your changes.

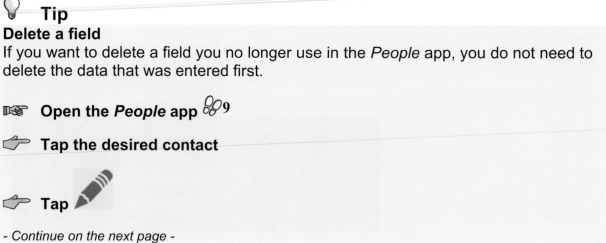

💡 **Tip**

Delete a field

If you want to delete a field you no longer use in the *People* app, you do not need to delete the data that was entered first.

☞ **Open the *People* app** 👣⁹

☞ **Tap the desired contact**

☞ **Tap** ✏️

- Continue on the next page -

☞ Tap ✕ by the field you want to delete ⎯

☞ Tap ✓ **DONE** ⎯

💡 **Tip**

Delete a contact

This is how to delete a contact in the *People* app:

☞ **Open the *People* app** 👣**9**

☞ **Tap the desired contact you want to remove**

☞ **Tap** ▮

☞ **Tap Delete**

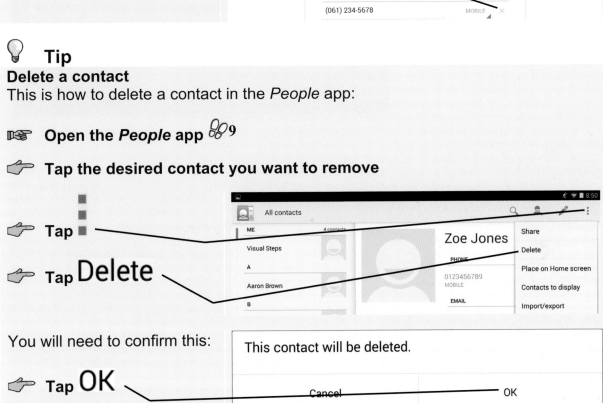

You will need to confirm this:

☞ **Tap OK**

💡 **Tip**

Find contacts

If you have a lot of contacts stored in the *People* app, it can get a little harder to find a contact quickly. Fortunately there is a useful search function to help you out:

☞ **Open the *People* app** 👣**9**

☞ **Tap** 🔍

- Continue on the next page -

Type the first letter of the first or last name

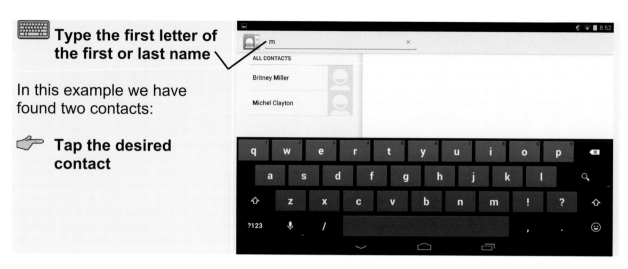

In this example we have found two contacts:

☞ **Tap the desired contact**

💡 **Tip**

Add a photo

If you have a photo stored of one of your contacts on your tablet, you can add it to the contact information for this person. In *Chapter 6 Photos, Videos and Music* you can read how to transfer photos to your tablet. This is how you add an existing photo to a contact's information:

☞ **Open the *People* app** 🦶[9]

☞ **Tap the desired contact**

☞ **Tap** ✏️

☞ **Tap**

☞ **Tap**
Choose photo from Gallery

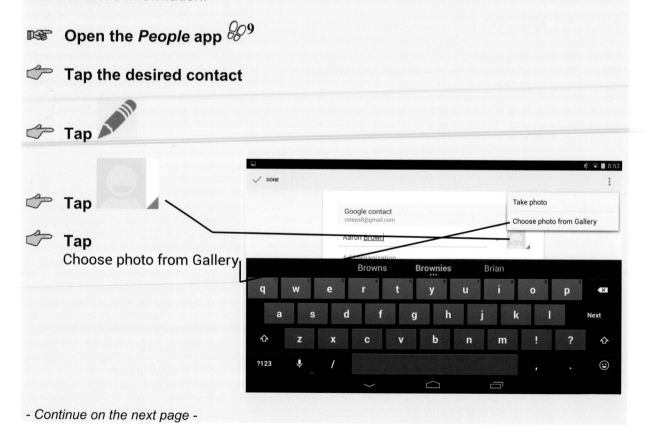

- Continue on the next page -

☞ **If necessary, tap**

☞ **If necessary, tap** 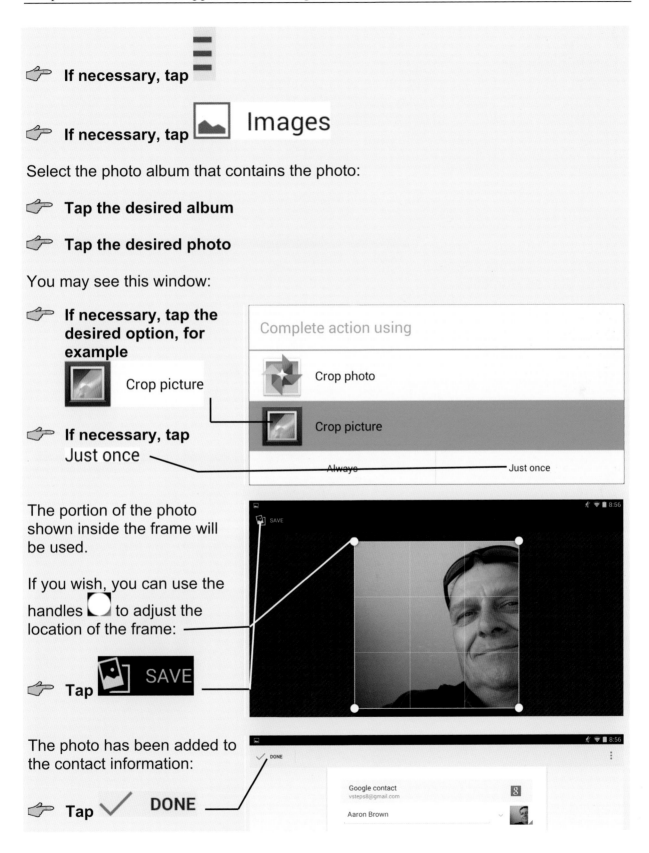 Images

Select the photo album that contains the photo:

☞ **Tap the desired album**

☞ **Tap the desired photo**

You may see this window:

☞ **If necessary, tap the desired option, for example**
Crop picture

Complete action using

Crop photo

Crop picture

Always   Just once

☞ **If necessary, tap**
Just once

The portion of the photo shown inside the frame will be used.

If you wish, you can use the handles to adjust the location of the frame:

☞ **Tap** SAVE

The photo has been added to the contact information:

☞ **Tap** ✓ DONE

Google contact
vsteps8@gmail.com

Aaron Brown

Tip

Share a calendar

You can use a *Google* calendar on various devices such as a computer or mobile device (smartphones and other types of tablets). But in order to share your *Google* calendar you will need to adjust a certain setting on the www.google.com/calendar website from your computer. Click the arrow ▼ next to your calendar and then click Share this Calendar.

If you use a shared calendar on your tablet, you can select the following options for an event:

If you use a shared calendar where others cannot see your events, you can indicate whether you are busy or free:

You can indicate whether the event is visible to others. The **Default** option will use the general privacy settings of the calendar:

 Tip

Edit or delete an event

If an event needs to be changed or has been cancelled, you can edit the event in the *Calendar* app, like this:

☞ **Tap the event**

☞ **Tap** 🖊

- Continue on the next page -

Now you will see the window in which you had originally entered the event. You can change the description, location, date or time of the event. After you have finished:

☞ **Tap** ✓ **DONE**

If you want to delete the event:

☞ **Tap** 🗑

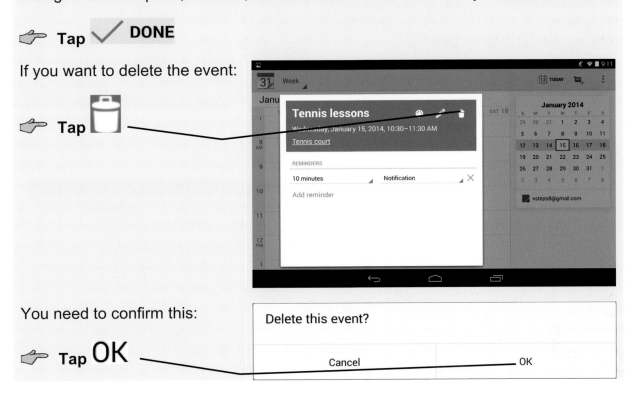

You need to confirm this:

Delete this event?

Cancel   OK

☞ **Tap OK**

💡 **Tip**
Import contacts
The contacts you have stored in your *Google* account will automatically be synchronized with all the other devices on which you use this *Google* account. If you already manage your contacts on your computer and use a different program, such as *Microsoft Outlook* or *Windows Live Mail*, you may be able to import these contacts to your tablet.

In order to import contacts on your tablet you need to have vCard files. You will need to use your email program to export and save the contacts to a folder with vCard files (these are files that have the .vcf file extension). Next, you can copy this folder to your tablet using *Windows Explorer*. If you need further information you can find this in the help function of the mail program you use.

Once the folder with the vCard files has been copied to your tablet, you can proceed as follows:

☞ **Open the *People* app** 🐾[9]

- Continue on the next page -

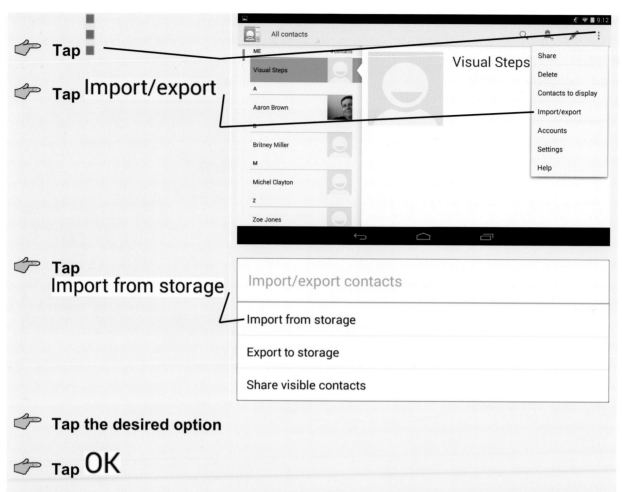

👉 **Tap** ■

👉 **Tap** Import/export

👉 **Tap**
   Import from storage

Import/export contacts
Import from storage
Export to storage
Share visible contacts

👉 **Tap the desired option**

👉 **Tap** OK

The contacts will be imported to your tablet. Remember, it is possible that some of the fields contained in the original contact data may not be imported.

 Tip

Turn off synchronization
The data in your *Google* account will automatically be synchronized with all the devices on which you use this *Google* account. This means that the information you have previously added to your account will also be displayed and used on your tablet. You can turn off this function for each individual app.

In this example we will turn off the synchronization for the calendar:

👉 **Open the *Settings* screen** 👣3

- Continue on the next page -

☞ **Drag upwards until you see ACCOUNTS**

☞ **By ACCOUNTS, tap**
8 Google

☞ **Tap your account**

☞ **Tap the checkmarks ☑ to delete them, by the apps you do not want to synchronize**

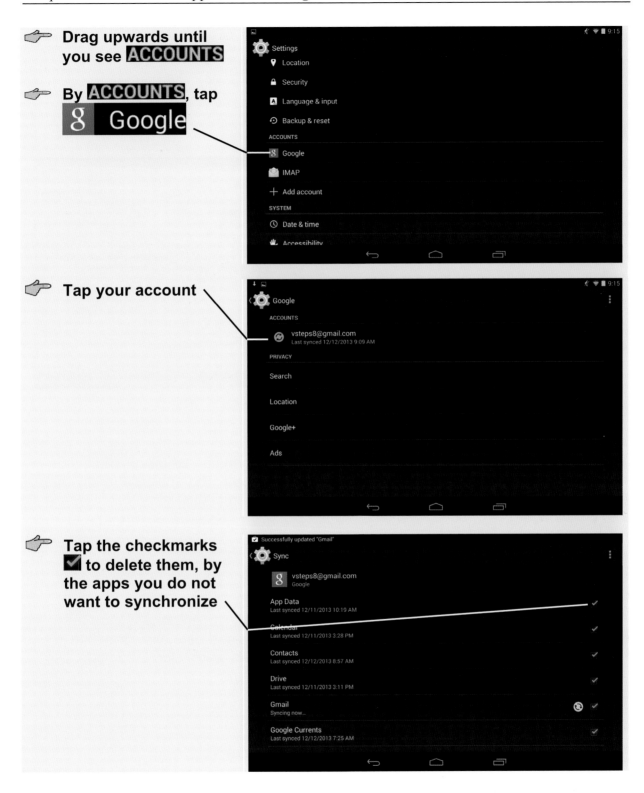

Tip

Traffic information

You can also display a layer with traffic information in the *Maps* app:

 Tap , **Traffic**

The traffic flows are displayed in a certain color:

Green: the traffic is moving along at a regular speed.

Yellow: traffic is moving slower than regular speed.

Red: traffic is moving very slowly.

 Tip

Apps overview

Your Google Nexus tablet contains many more apps than can be discussed in this book. Below you will find a brief description of these apps. The apps that are discusses in the next couple of chapters are not included in this list.

 Calculator.

 With this app you can see the current time and date, view the time in different parts of the world, and use it as an alarm clock. You can also use this app as a timer and a stopwatch.

 A social magazine app that presents the news.

Downloads

This app provides direct access to the folder containing the file sthat have been downloaded to the tablet. You can also use this app to send downloaded files. See the *Tip* at the back of this chapter for additional information.

Drive

The *Drive* app is a cloud storage service from *Google*. You can store photos, videos and documents there and access them whereever you are on other mobile devices or computers. You can also share files with others.

Earth

An app that can find virtually any place in the world. This app offers more features than *Google Maps*, especially with regard to viewing buildings, images, and surroundings in 3D.

Google Settings

In this app you can change a number of settings that apply to *Google* only.

Google+

A social network site from *Google*, comparable to *Facebook*. It requires a *Google* account in order to use it and to create a profile.

Hangouts

This app allows you to start a video conversation and send photos to other people who also use *Google Hangouts*. You need to be connected to the Internet and have a *Google* account in order to use the app. Your contact also needs to have a *Google* account and be a *Google Hangouts* user.

Keep

This handy app allows you to keep notes and set reminders. You can also create checklists and enter voice notes with this app.

Make and manage your photos with the *Photos* app.

App to read e-books on your tablet.

The *Play Games* app lets you discover new games and it keeps track of your scores. You can also use it to play games with other people.

The *Play Newsstand* app lets you read magazines and newspapers all in one place on your tablet.

You can create documents, spreadsheets and presentations with *Quickoffice*. Then you can edit them further in *Microsoft Office* on a pc later on, if you wish.

With this app you can use *Google Search* to search your tablet or the Internet by speaking aloud instead of typing.

An app with which you can watch videos on *YouTube*.

Tip

Widgets

Besides apps you will also find widgets on your tablet. Actually, widgets are tiny, interactive programs that are often related to another app. You can move these widgets to the Home screen.

 **Tap**

 **Tap** WIDGETS

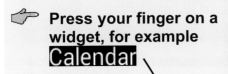 **Press your finger on a widget, for example Calendar**

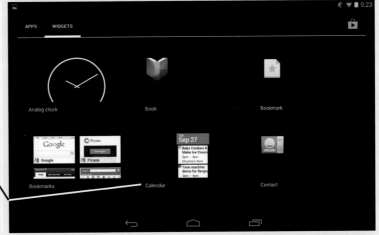

- Continue on the next page -

The Home screen will be
opened:

 Release the widget

Now you can see the widget
on your Home screen: ─────

In this example you see the
Calendar widget, and you
can see that there are no
events planned.

This is how you remove a
widget from the Home
screen:

 **Press your finger on
the widget**

 Drag the widget to ─

 Release the screen

Tip

Notifications

In the top left-hand corner of your screen you will constantly see different icons. These icons are used to indicate notifications about a new email message, calendar or other event, for instance.

Here you see the notification icons: ────────

 Drag downwards from the top left-hand corner of the screen

You will see the notifications:

Tap the icon to the left of the notification to go to the corresponding app:

You can delete a notification by dragging it away.

To delete all notifications, tap

 :

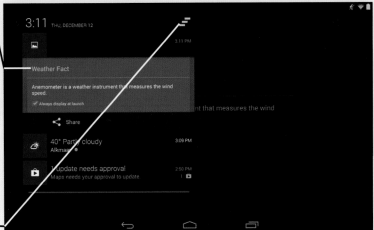

 Tip

Google Now

Google Now is an extension of the *Google Search* app. You could say *Google Now* is a kind of personal assistant. You can get information any time you like, for instance, about the weather, traffic conditions, your appointments and even special places of interest. *Google Now* uses your personal data, such as your location, calendar and browser history to gather this information (provided these services have been enabled).

If *Google Now* has not been turned on yet, you need to make a setting change first:

 Open the *Google Search* app 🐾**9**

- Continue on the next page -

First you need to drag the
keyboard downwards:

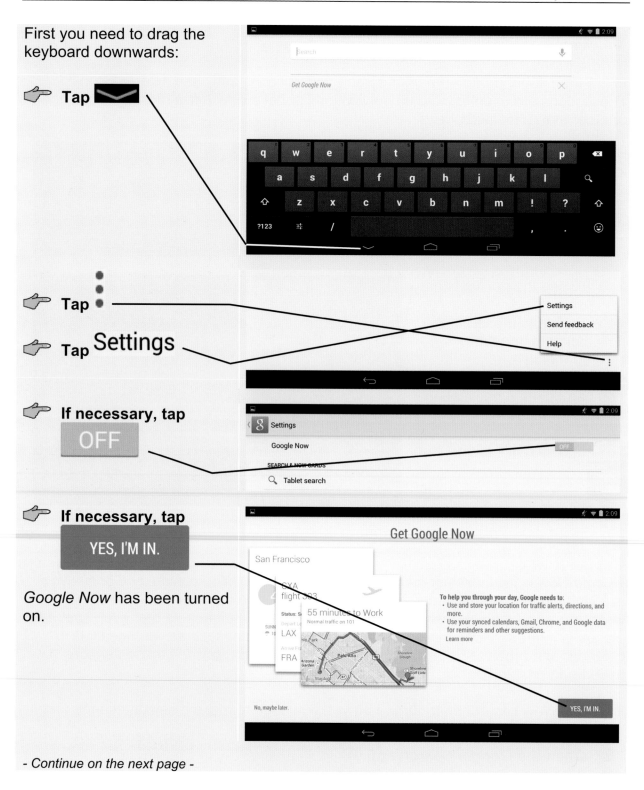

☞ **Tap**

☞ **Tap**

☞ **Tap Settings**

☞ **If necessary, tap**
OFF

☞ **If necessary, tap**
YES, I'M IN.

Google Now has been turned
on.

- Continue on the next page -

You will see the weather forecast for your current location, among other things

To view more information:

☞ **Drag the screen downwards**

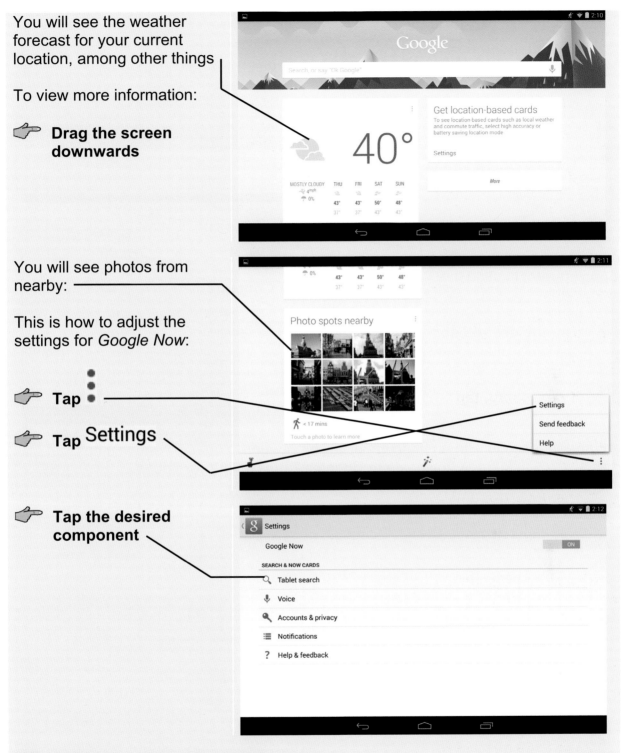

You will see photos from nearby:

This is how to adjust the settings for *Google Now*:

☞ **Tap** ⋮

☞ **Tap** Settings

☞ **Tap the desired component**

☞ **Select the desired option(s)**

The more you use *Google Now* on your tablet, the better *Google Now* will be able to inform you about various items.

Tip
Send downloaded documents
In the *Downloads* app you can send documents you have downloaded on your tablet. You can do that like this:

☞ **Open the *Downloads* app** ⁹

☞ **Tap the document you want to send**

☞ **Tap** ◁

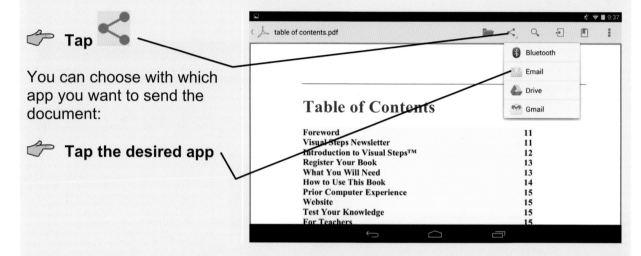

You can choose with which app you want to send the document:

☞ **Tap the desired app**

An email message with an attachment will be opened. You can send this email in the same way you learned how to do in *Chapter 2 Email On Your Tablet*.

5. Downloading Apps

In the previous chapters you have learned how to use the standard apps on your Google Nexus tablet. But there are many other apps available that will provide extra functionality to your tablet. In the *Play Store* you can find thousands of apps for free and paid which you can download and install.

There are far too many apps to list them all here. There are apps for news and magazines, the weather, games, recipes, travel information and even sports results. You are sure to find something interesting in the *Play Store*.

In this chapter you will learn how to download a free app from the *Play Store*. If you want to purchase an app you will need to link a credit card account to your *Google* account. You can do this in just a few easy steps, if you wish.

Once you have purchased several apps, you can re-arrange the order of the apps as they appear on your tablet to your own liking by moving them around. You can also create folders to store apps. And you can delete the apps you no longer use.

In this chapter you will learn how to:

- download and install a free app;
- link a credit card to your *Google* account;
- buy and install an app;
- move apps;
- store apps in a folder;
- delete apps.

 Please note:

In order to buy and download apps in the *Play Store* you need to have linked a *Google* account to your tablet. If you do not yet have a *Google* account, you can read how to create one in *section 1.6 Creating and Adding a Google Account*.

5.1 Downloading a Free App

In the *Play Store* you will find thousands of free apps. This is how you open the *Play Store*:

☞ **Unlock or turn on your tablet** ⚚¹

☞ **Tap**

☞ **Tap** Play Store

The *Play Store* is opened. You will be signed in automatically with your *Google* account:

To use *Google Play*, you will need to accept the terms of service first, if you have not already done so:

By using Google Play, you agree to the Google Play Terms of Service.

☑ Keep me up to date with news and offers from Google Play.

Decline   Accept

☞ **If necessary, tap** Accept

☞ **Tap** APPS

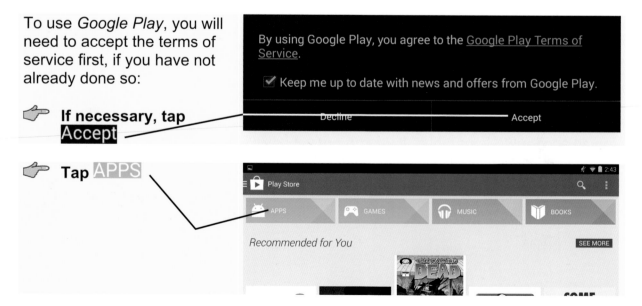

You will see the **HOME** webpage where a number of new apps are highlighted:

☞ Tap **CATEGORIES**

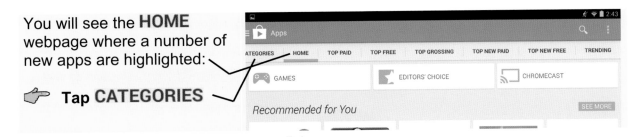

A list is shown with available apps, arranged by category:

☞ **Drag the list upwards until you see** Weather

☞ **Tap** Weather

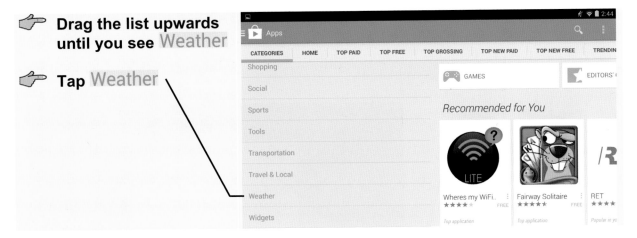

Now you see a page with highlighted apps in the *Weather* category. This is how you go to the free apps in this category:

☞ Tap **TOP FREE**

You will see all sorts of free apps regarding the weather. Take a look at a popular free app:

☞ **Drag the list upwards until you see**

☞ **Tap the app**

Now you will see a window with more information about this app. This is how to download the app:

☞ Tap INSTALL

You will see the permissions the app needs in order to work properly on your tablet. You need to accept these permissions:

☞ Tap ACCEPT

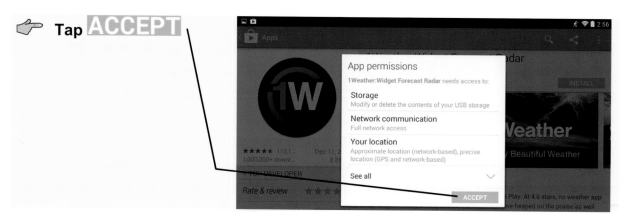

The app will be installed:

Here you see the progress of the download and install procedures:

When the app has been installed, you can open it from this page:

☞ Tap OPEN

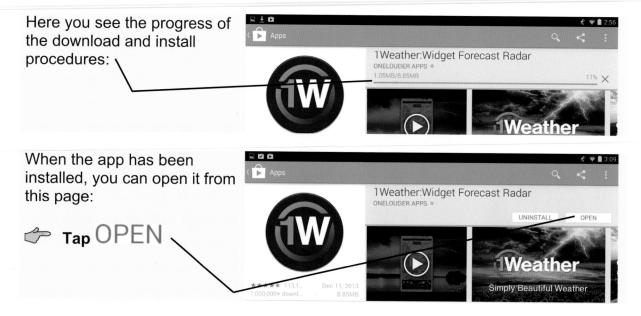

The *1Weather* app will first show a window containing a weather fact:

☞ **Tap** **OK**

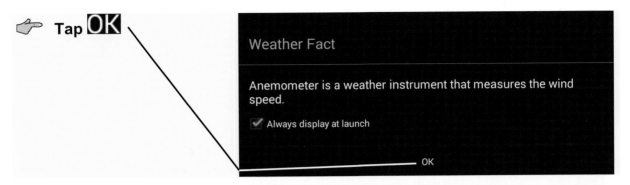

Here you see the *1Weather* app:

☞ **Go back to the Home screen** 👣²

💡 **Tip**

Manage apps
The new app will automatically be placed on the Home screen. And the app will also be listed in the apps overview. In *section 5.3 Managing Apps* you can read how to arrange the apps in a different order.

In the next section you will learn how to purchase an app.

5.2 Downloading a Paid App

If you want to download and install a paid app, you will need to pay for this app by credit card. When you try to download a paid app, you will be asked to link a credit card account to your *Google* account.

If you do not (yet) have a credit card you can just read through this section.

HELP! I do not have a credit card.

At the time we were writing this book, the only payment method in the *Play Store* was by credit card. If you do not have a credit card you could consider buying a prepaid credit card for about $10.00, for instance at http://www.mastercard.us/prepaid-card.html or http://usa.visa.com/personal/cards/prepaid/index.html.

But there are lots of other prepaid credit cards you can purchase. The card fees for these credit cards will vary. These types of credit cards can be 'loaded' with any amount you like. With a prepaid credit card you can only pay for something if you have previously loaded the card with a certain amount of money. This means there is less risk involved when you pay for online purchases.

☞ **Open the *Play Store* app** 👣⁹

You will probably still be looking at the page with the *1Weather* app. This is how you go back to the *Play Store*:

☞ **Tap**

Previously, you have searched for an app through the various categories. But you can also search directly for the name of the app you want to download:

☞ **Tap**

In this example we will look for the name of a game:

⌨ **Type:** super bee

☞ **Tap**

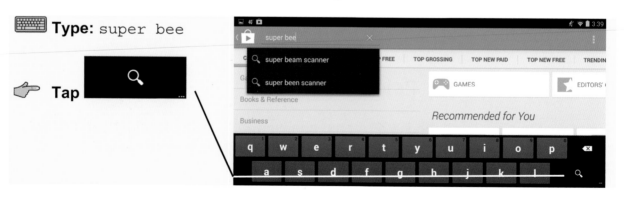

This is a paid app. In the following section you will see how to purchase this app:

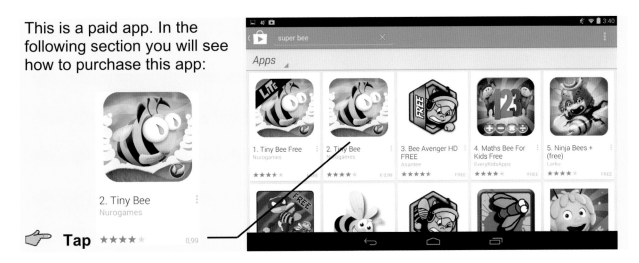

2. Tiny Bee
Nurogames

 Tap ★★★★☆ 0,99

⤵ Please note:

In the next example we will buy an app. You can decide for yourself whether you want to follow these steps and purchase an app. Of course, you do not have to purchase the same app as in this example. After you have ordered an app you can still cancel the order within fifteen minutes. You can find more information on this subject in the *Tip* on page 155.

⤵ Please note:

You can only follow the next steps if you link a credit card to your *Google* account. If you do not (yet) have a credit card, or if you do not want to enter your credit card information, you can just read through this section.

The app we are going to purchase in this example costs $ 0.99:

 Tap 0.99

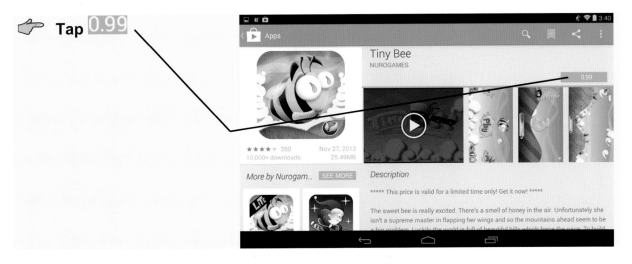

You will see the window with the required authorizations for this app. You need to accept these permissions:

☞ **Tap** ACCEPT

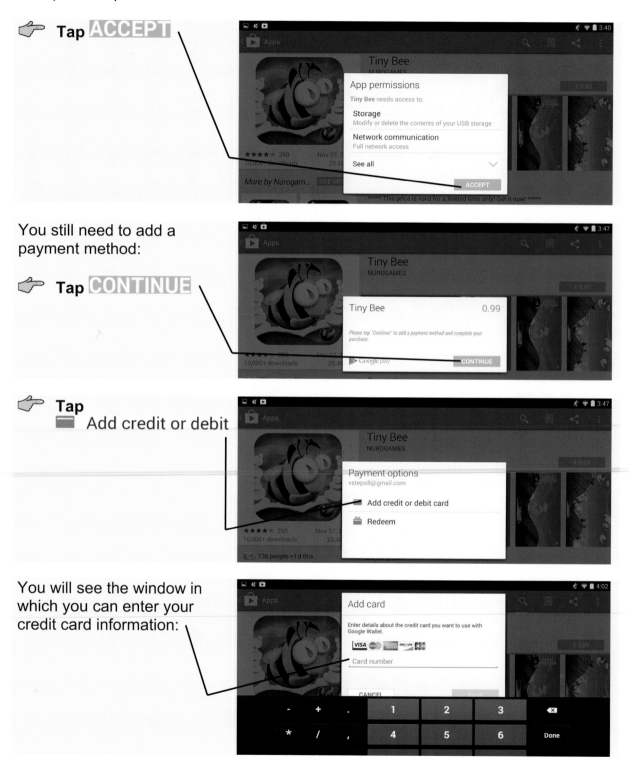

You still need to add a payment method:

☞ **Tap** CONTINUE

☞ **Tap** 🔲 Add credit or debit

You will see the window in which you can enter your credit card information:

Type your credit card information and your name

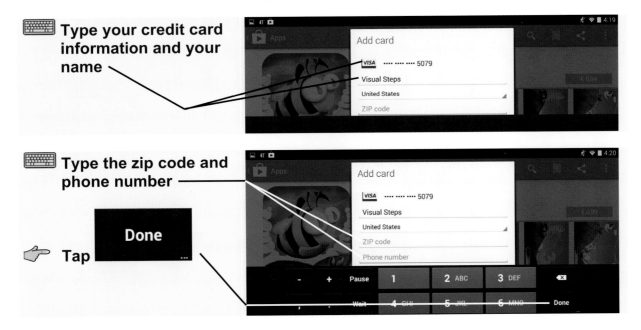

Type the zip code and phone number

☞ **Tap** Done

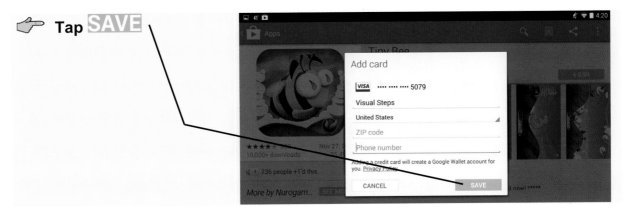

If all the data has been entered correctly:

☞ **Tap** SAVE

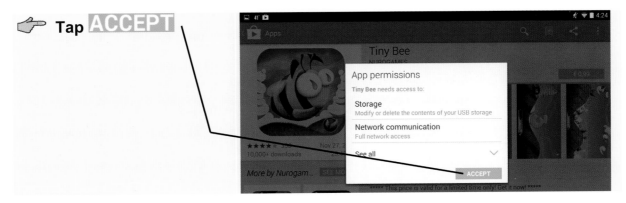

First, you will need to agree to the terms and conditions of service:

☞ **Tap** ACCEPT

☞ **Tap BUY**

You need to confirm your purchase with the password of your *Google*-account.

⌨ **Type your password**

☞ **Tap CONFIRM**

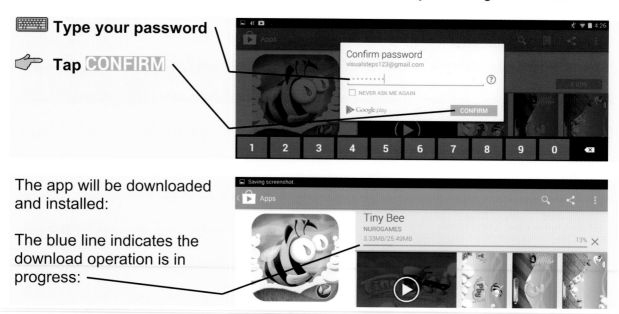

The app will be downloaded and installed:

The blue line indicates the download operation is in progress:

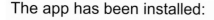

After the app has been downloaded you will receive an email from *Google Play*. You will hear a sound signal and see a message in the top left-hand corner of your screen.

The app has been installed:

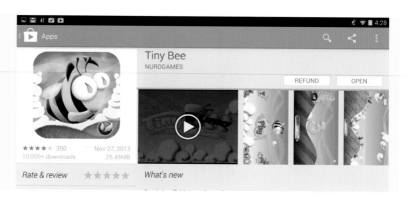

Go back to the *Play Store* Home screen:

☞ **Tap**

Later on, you can take a look at the app you just downloaded.

☞ **Go back to the Home screen** 👣**2**

💡 **Tip**

Cancel an order

You can still cancel the purchase of an app within fifteen minutes after ordering it. This is handy if you find that you do not like the app after all. To start the refund procedure:

☞ **Open the *Play Store* app** 👣**9**

To view the installed apps:

☞ **Tap**

☞ **Tap** My apps

☞ **If necessary, drag upwards to see the new app**

☞ **Tap the app**

☞ **Tap REFUND**

Please note: after fifteen minutes this button will have disappeared.

☞ **Tap Yes**

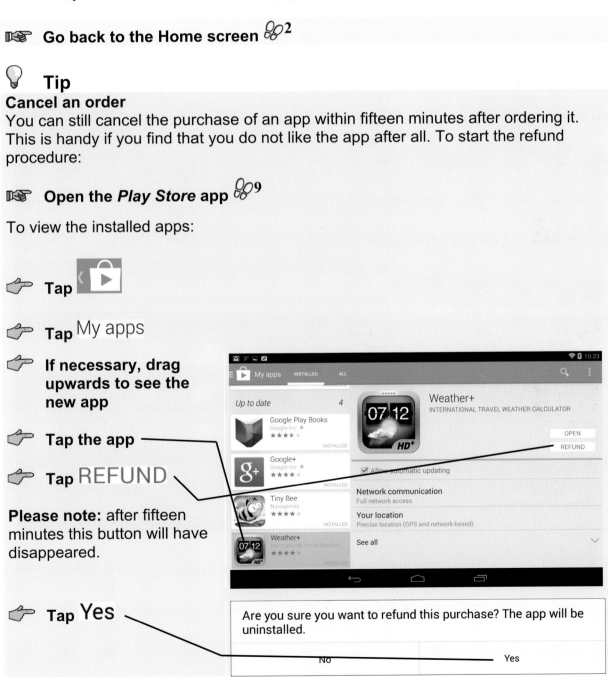

5.3 Managing Apps

You can arrange the installed apps in the order you prefer by moving them.

 Please note:

To be able to do the following steps, you will need to have installed at least two apps. If you have not purchased any paid apps, then download one more free app, as described in *section 5.1 Downloading a Free App*.

You will see the installed apps on the Home screen:

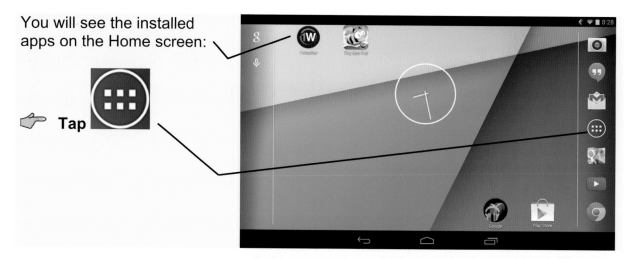

☞ **Tap**

The new apps are also included in the apps overview. If the app you are looking for is not shown on this screen, drag your finger over the screen from right to left to see the next page of apps.

The apps are placed in alphabetical order. You cannot change this.

☞ **Go back to the Home screen** 🐾²

You can arrange the apps any way you want to. This is how you move an app:

☞ **Press your finger on the app**

☞ **Drag the app to a different spot** ———

☞ **Release the app**

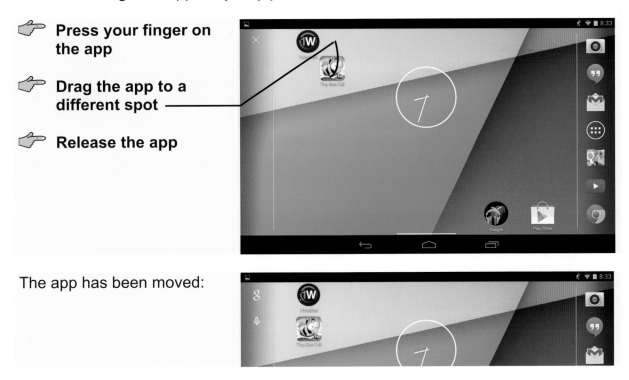

The app has been moved:

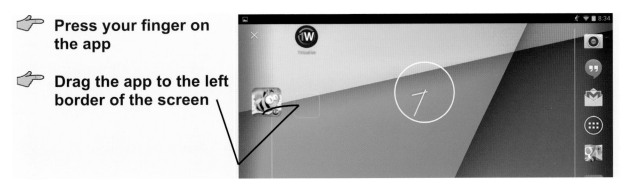

You can also move the app to another page. This is how you move the app to another page:

☞ **Press your finger on the app**

☞ **Drag the app to the left border of the screen**

When you see the other page:

☞ **Release the app**

Now the app has been moved to another page:

To go back to the previous page:

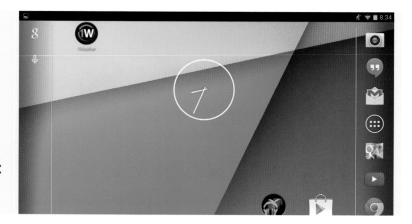

 Drag across the screen from left to right

 Move the second app to the page on the left as well $\mathcal{GO}$ **10**

You can also store apps in a folder. This is how you do it:

 Press your finger on an app

 Drag the app on top of the other app

When you see a blue circle around the other app:

 Release the app

Now the app has been moved to a folder:

 Tap the folder

The folder is opened:

You can enter a name for this folder:

 Tap Unnamed Fold

⌨ Type a name

☞ Tap Done

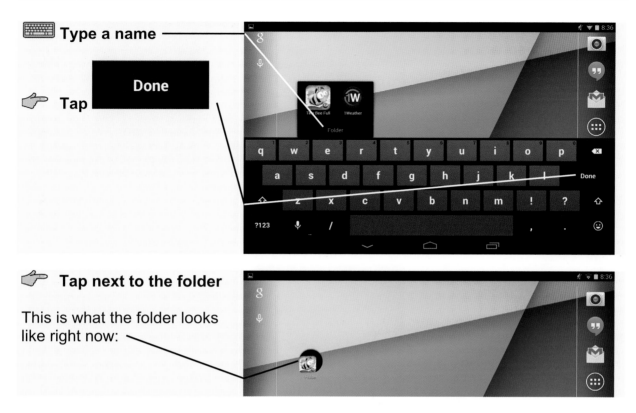

☞ Tap next to the folder

This is what the folder looks like right now:

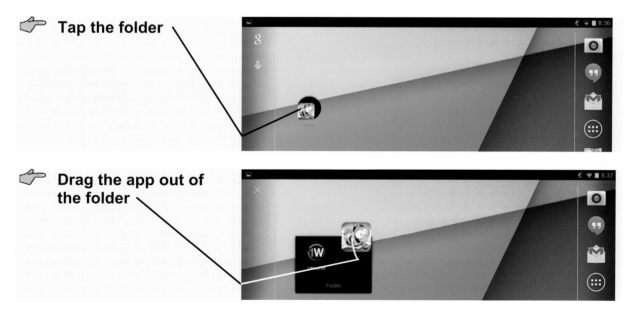

You can add even more apps to the folder. You do this by dragging apps into the folder.

This is how you remove an app from the folder:

☞ Tap the folder

☞ Drag the app out of the folder

You will see that the folder has disappeared, all by itself. This is because there was just a single app left in the folder. A folder needs to contain more than one app.

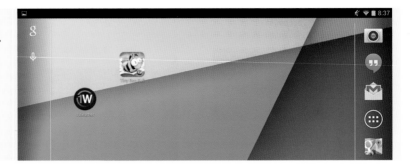

To keep your Home screen uncluttered, you may want to remove the apps from the Home screen altogether, since they are already included in the apps overview. This is how you remove an app from the Home screen:

 **Press your finger on the app**

You will see an ⊠ in the top left-hand corner:

 **Drag the app to the** ⊠

 **Release the app**

The app has been removed from the Home screen:

 Remove the other app from the Home screen too ✂^{11}

⤵ Please note:

In the previous steps, the apps have been removed from the Home screen but not from your tablet. They will still be visible in the apps overview. In the next section we will explain how to delete an app from your tablet.

5.4 Deleting an App

If you have downloaded an app and it is not to your liking, you can delete it. You do this using the *Play Store*.

You will see the list of installed apps. You can delete the apps you have downloaded from the *Play Store*:

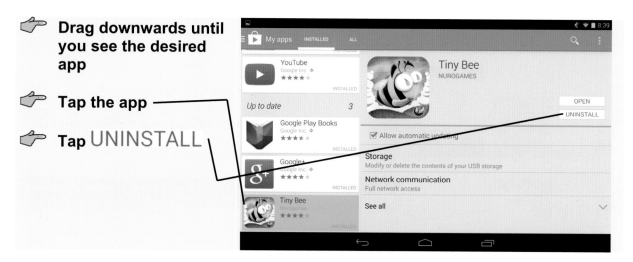

☞ **Drag downwards until you see the desired app**

☞ **Tap the app**

☞ **Tap** UNINSTALL

If you really want to delete the app:

☞ **Tap** OK

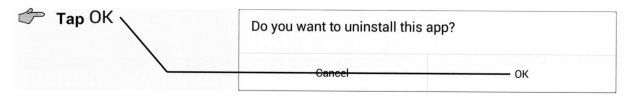

Do you want to uninstall this app?

Cancel   OK

The app will be deleted from your tablet.

☞ **Go back to the Home screen** 𝒪𝒪²

☞ **Lock or turn off your tablet, if you wish** 𝒪𝒪⁵

In this chapter you have learned how to download free and paid apps in the *Play Store*. You have also learned how to arrange the apps on your Home screen and how to delete an app you no longer want.

5.5 Background Information

Dictionary

App   Short for *application*, a program for the tablet.

Favorites tray   On the Home screen you can find the Favorites tray. By using this tray you can quickly navigate to your apps, books, music, etcetera.

Google account   A combination of an email address and a password. You need to have a *Google* account in order to download apps from the *Play Store*.

Google Play widgets   Recommendations by *Google Play*, placed on the Home screen.

Play Store   An online store where you can download free and paid apps.

Source: Google Nexus tablet User Guide

5.6 Tips

 Tip

Update apps

The apps you have installed on your tablet will occasionally offer free updates. These updates may be essential for solving certain problems (often called bug fixes). An update may also add new features and options to an app, such as a new game level. This is how you check for updates:

☞ **Open the** *Play Store* **app** ⁹

☞ **Tap**

☞ **Tap** My apps

To update all the apps:

☞ **Tap** UPDATE ALL

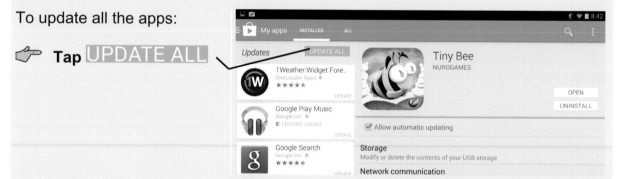

If you only want to update a specific app:

☞ **Tap the app**

☞ **Tap** UPDATE

☞ **Tap** CONTINUE **or** ACCEPT

The updates will be downloaded and installed. This may take a few minutes.

- Continue on the next page -

The apps have been updated. There are no other updates available:

You can select Allow automatic updating per app:

Then the update will be installed as soon as it becomes available:

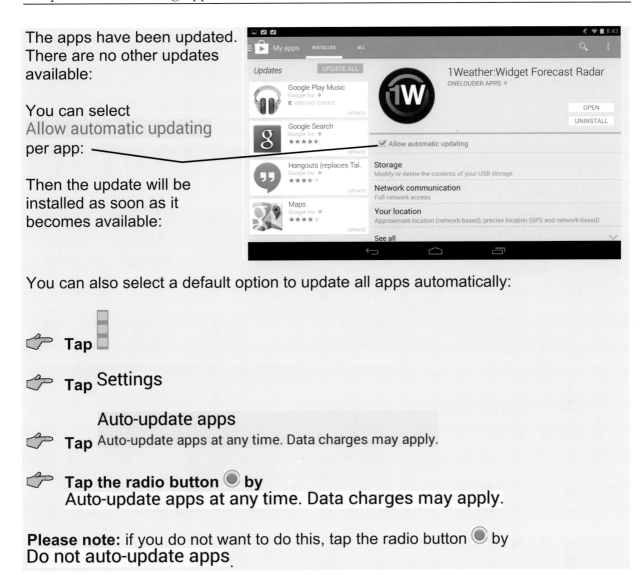

You can also select a default option to update all apps automatically:

 **Tap**

 **Tap** Settings

 Auto-update apps
 **Tap** Auto-update apps at any time. Data charges may apply.

 **Tap the radio button ◉ by**
 Auto-update apps at any time. Data charges may apply.

Please note: if you do not want to do this, tap the radio button ◉ by
Do not auto-update apps.

💡 **Tip**

Social media
Are you active on *Facebook* or *Twitter*? On the Google Nexus tablet you can

download apps which will let you use *Facebook* 🅵 and *Twitter* 🐦. Find these apps in the *Play Store* and download them as instructed in *section 5.1 Downloading a Free App*. Once these apps have been installed on your tablet, you can use them to update your friends and family about your latest activities.

Tip

Download a paid app once more

If you have deleted a paid app by mistake or otherwise, you can still download it again for free. You need to use the same *Google* account originally used to purchase the app to do this.

The app has been checked ✅:

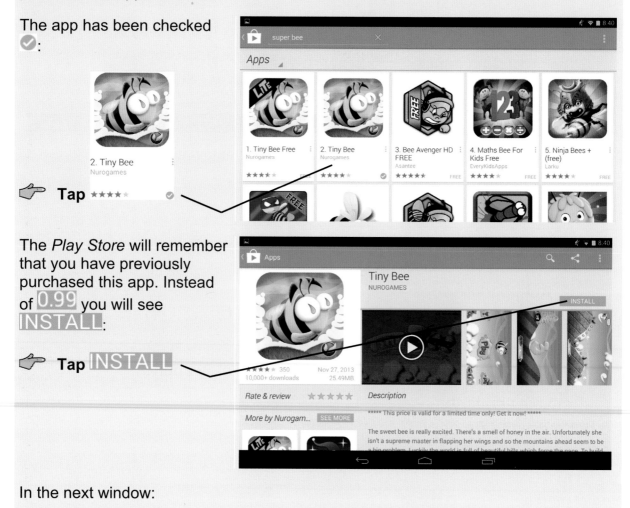

☞ **Tap** ★★★★★

The *Play Store* will remember that you have previously purchased this app. Instead of 0.99 you will see INSTALL:

☞ **Tap** INSTALL

In the next window:

☞ **Tap** ACCEPT

The app will be downloaded and installed. The download will not be charged to your account.

Tip

Adjust the Favorites tray
You can find the Favorites tray on the right-hand side or at the bottom of each screen. You can move and replace the apps in the Favorites tray as well. This is done in the same way as you move the other apps on the Home screen.

In this example you are going to delete an app from the Favorites tray:

☞ **Press your finger on the desired app**

☞ **Drag the app to the Home screen, or to** ⊠

☞ **Release the app**

You can also move an app from the Home screen to the Favorites tray:

☞ **Press your finger on the desired app**

☞ **Drag the app to the Favorites tray**

☞ **Release the app**

- Continue on the next page -

The app has been added to the Favorites tray:

The Home screen or Favorites tray contains a folder too:

You can manage this folder in the same way as you manage a folder on the Home screen. You can add apps to the folder, or remove them. You can also delete the entire folder.

 Tip
Google Play widgets
On the right-hand page of the Home screen you will find the *Google Play* widgets. These are recommendations made by the *Play Store*. By tapping a widget you will launch the *Play Store,* where you can view more information and purchase the app if you wish. You can open the right-hand page by dragging across the screen from right to left.

☞ **Drag across the screen from right to left**

If you want to disable similar recommendations in the future, tap :

To view another recommendation tap :

This is how you delete a widget from the Home screen:

☞ **Press your finger to the widget**

☞ **Drag the widget to** ⊠

☞ **Release the widget**

6. Photos, Videos and Music

You can copy photos, videos and music to your Google Nexus tablet. Then you can view these files or listen to them on your tablet. You can also use your tablet to send photos by email.

The Google Nexus tablet is equipped with two cameras that will give you plenty of opportunity for taking pictures or shooting videos. The *Camera* app lets you use the built-in rear-facing camera so you can take a picture or record a video of an interesting object. With the camera on the front you can shoot self-portraits, for example. Please note: the first generation Google Nexus tablet is not equipped with a rear-facing camera. See for more information the next page.

You can use the *Gallery* app to view photos and videos. You can view them one by one or display them as a slideshow on your tablet.

To listen to your music, you can use the *Play Music* app.

In this chapter you will get acquainted with all of these useful apps.

In this chapter you will learn how to:

- take pictures;
- switch between the cameras on the front and back;
- record a video;
- view photos;
- zoom in and zoom out of photos;
- view a slideshow;
- send a photo by email;
- copy photos, videos and music to your tablet;
- watch a video;
- play music.

 Please note:

In order to follow the examples in this chapter you will need to have multiple photo, video and music files saved on your computer. If you do not have any multimedia files or you are missing a particular file format, you can just read through this chapter or skip to a section that applies to the types of files you do have.

6.1 Taking Pictures

You can use the *Camera* app to take pictures. This is how you open the app:

☞ **If necessary, unlock or turn on your tablet** 👣¹

👉 Tap

👉 Tap Camera

✖ HELP! I do not have the Camera app on my tablet.

Older versions of the Google Nexus tablet only have a front-facing camera. This type of camera is mainly used for video chatting. But you can still make a good enough photo or video with this camera. Since the camera app is not one of the default apps, you will need to download and install a new app from the *Play Store*. In *Chapter 5. Downloading apps* you can read how to download and install an app. In the *Play Store*, search with the words: camera nexus 7 to find the app.

Please note: this is a front-facing camera. Not all the options in this chapter are possible.

When the app opens you may see a message asking you about your current location. If you want, you can allow this information to be used. Then your photos will also contain the location (geo tagging information) of where the pictures were taken:

👉 **If necessary, tap** Yes

Now you will see the image that is captured by the camera on the back of the Google Nexus.

 Point the camera towards the object you want to photograph

Please note:
Make sure there is enough light. The Google Nexus tablet 7 does not have a flash. If you take pictures in poor lighting conditions, the photos will look grainy.

This is how you take the picture:

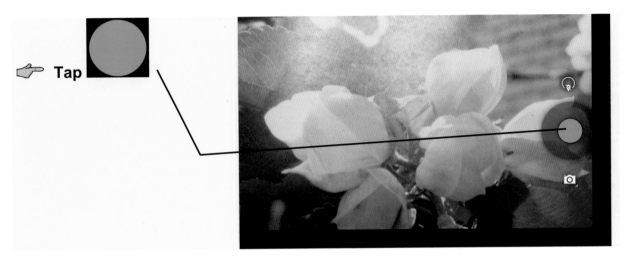

☞ **Tap**

The photo will be stored on your tablet.

 Make some more pictures 🦶¹⁴

Tip

Self-portrait
You can also use the camera on the front of the tablet. This makes it possible to take a picture of yourself. Here is how to switch to the camera on the front:

☞ **Tap** ,

You will see the image captured by the camera on the front. Now you can take a picture, in the same way as you did previously with the camera on the back.

- Continue on the next page -

You can switch back to the rear-facing camera like this:

☞ **Tap** ,

If you tap you will see other buttons on the screen of the *Camera* app. They have the following functions:

Button	Description
	Tap this button if you want to record a video with your tablet.
	Tap this button to create a panorama photo. You start by tapping the blue button, and then slowly move the tablet horizontally. Then tap the blue button once more to stop.
	Tap this button to create a photo sphere. This function allows you to take a series of photos that will be turned into a seamless 360 degree panorama or a wide angle shot. Tap the blue button to start and adjust the camera angle so the blue dot is centered inside the doughnut. Pan or tilt until the circle in the center of the screen moves over a white dot and records that portion of the image. Keep moving over the white dots until you're finished, and then tap the blue button to stop.

If you tap you will see other buttons on the screen of the *Camera* app. They have the following functions:

Button	Description
	Use this button to adjust the exposure, contrast, shadows, and so on.
	Use this button to adjust a variety of settings. You can enable or disable location information, adjust the picture size and set a countdown timer.
	Use this button to switch between the front-facing camera and the rear-facing camera.

6.2 Recording a Video

You can also use the camera to record a video:

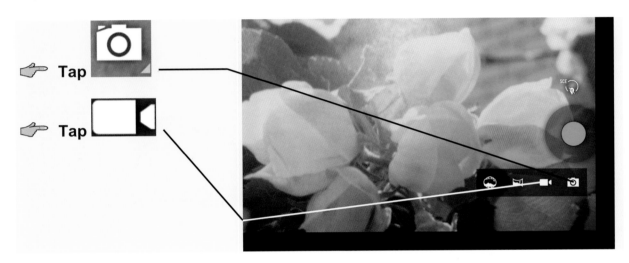

☞ **Tap**

☞ **Tap**

💡 **Tip**

Sideways

Would you like to watch your video on television or on a monitor later on? Then turn your tablet sideways so it is in landscape mode. This way, you will capture a nice full-screen image.

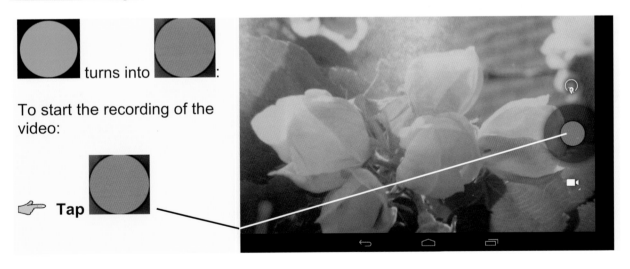

turns into   :

To start the recording of the video:

☞ **Tap**

To stop the recording:

☞ **Tap**

Now you can set the *Camera* app to take pictures again:

☞ **Tap**

☞ **Tap**

☞ **Go back to the Home screen** 🐾²

6.3 Viewing Photos in the Gallery

Once you have taken a few pictures, you will probably want to view them. You can do this with the *Gallery* app. Here is how you open the *Gallery* app:

☞ **Tap** , Gallery

You will see one or more albums:

👉 **Tap the album with the photos**

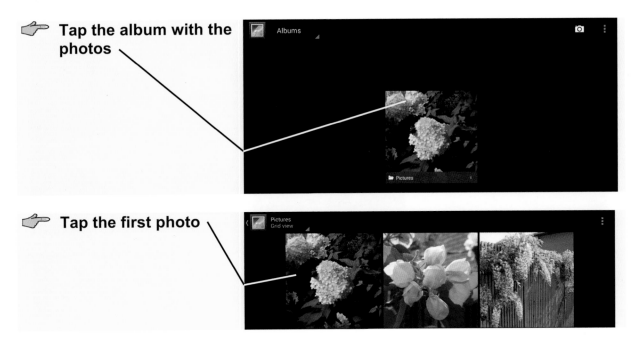

👉 **Tap the first photo**

The photo will be displayed full-screen. This is how you skip to the next photo:

👉 **Swipe across the photo, from right to left**

You will see the next photo.

👉 **Swipe across the photo, from right to left**

You will see the third photo. You can also zoom in on a photo. For this, you will need to use the touch gestures you previously used while surfing the Internet:

 **Spread your thumb and index finger, across the screen**

You will zoom in on the photo:

 Tip

Move
You can also move the photo by dragging your finger across the screen.

This is how you zoom out again:

 Move your thumb and index finger towards each other, across the screen (pinch)

You will see the regular view of the photo again:

This is how you go back to the first photo:

☞ **Swipe across the photo twice, from left to right**

You can also watch a slideshow of all the photos in an album. You do that like this:

☞ **Tap the photo**

☞ **Tap** ▫

☞ **Tap**
Slideshow

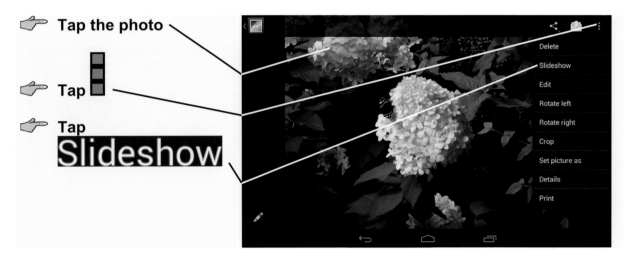

You will see the slideshow. This is how you stop the slideshow:

☞ **Tap the screen**

The last photo displayed in the slideshow will freeze on the screen.

💡 **Tip**
Delete a photo
You can use *File Explorer* on your computer to delete a photo. But you can also use your tablet to delete a photo, like this:

☞ **Tap the photo**

☞ **Tap** ▫

☞ Tap Delete

6.4 Sending a Photo by Email

If you have a nice picture stored on your tablet, you can share it by adding it to an email message. The photo you want to share needs to be opened on the tablet:

☞ **If necessary, open the photo you want to share** 🦶[12]

👉 **Tap the photo**

👉 **Tap**

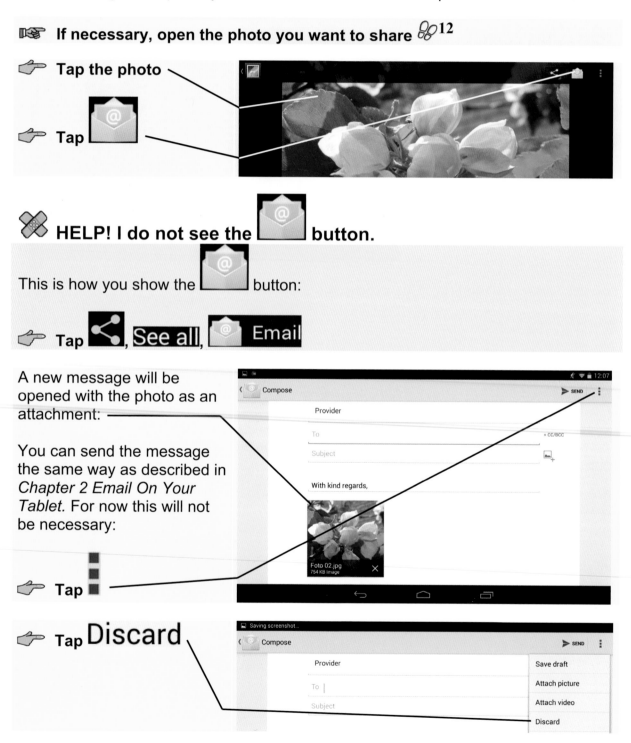

🩹 **HELP! I do not see the** ✉ **button.**

This is how you show the ✉ button:

👉 **Tap** ⁍, **See all**, ✉ **Email**

A new message will be opened with the photo as an attachment:

You can send the message the same way as described in *Chapter 2 Email On Your Tablet.* For now this will not be necessary:

👉 **Tap** ▪

👉 **Tap** Discard

You will be asked if you really want to discard the message:

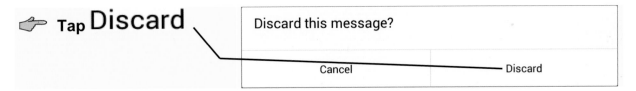

👉 **Tap** **Discard**

Discard this message?

Cancel   Discard

You will see the photo again.

☞ **Go back to the Home screen** 𝒬ℓ²

6.5 Copying Photos, Videos and Music to Your Tablet

The photo, video and music you have saved on your computer can be copied to your tablet using *File Explorer*.

🢆 **Please note:**

The Google Nexus tablet does not support all available file formats. However, it does support the following formats:

Photo files   JPEG, GIF, PNG, BMP, and WEBP

Video files   MPEG-4/MP4, H.263, H.264 AVC, and VP8

Music files   MP3, AAC, FLAC, MIDI, PCM/WAVE, Vorbis, AMR-WB, and AMR-NB

If you have a video file of the AVI file type, you can convert it to a MP4 file. To do this, you can use free conversion programs such as *Freemake Video Converter* and *Any Video Converter Free*. With these programs you can also convert photo and music files.

Another option is to find and download a new app. In the *Play Store* you can find many apps that can play AVI files.

☞ **Connect your tablet to the computer**

☞ **If necessary, close the *AutoPlay* window** 𝒬ℓ⁸

In this example we use screen shots from a computer running *Windows 8*. If you are using a different *Windows* version you will see similar windows.

You open *File Explorer* on your desktop. In *Windows 8* on the Start screen:

Click the Desktop tile

In all *Windows* versions:

In the bottom left-hand corner of the desktop:

Click

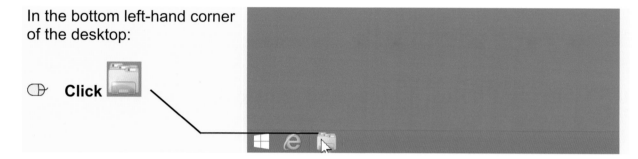

Now you are going to copy a number of photos to your tablet. First, you open the folder where your pictures are stored:

Click the Pictures library

If necessary, double-click the folder that contains the photos

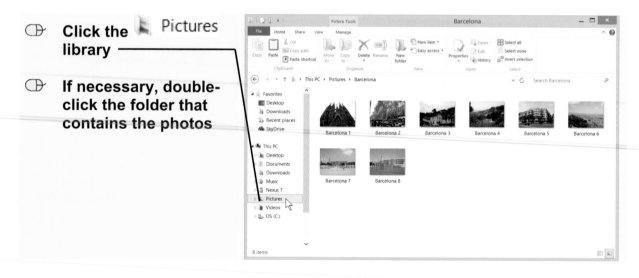

You will see the photos that have been saved on your computer. You may see lots of other photos and possibly sub-folders as well. The next few actions can be performed using your own photos. You will be selecting multiple photos and copying them to your tablet:

Click the first photo

Press the **Shift** **key and hold it down**

Click the last photo

To select photos that are not placed next to each other,

you use the **Ctrl** key instead.

Right-click a photo

Click Copy

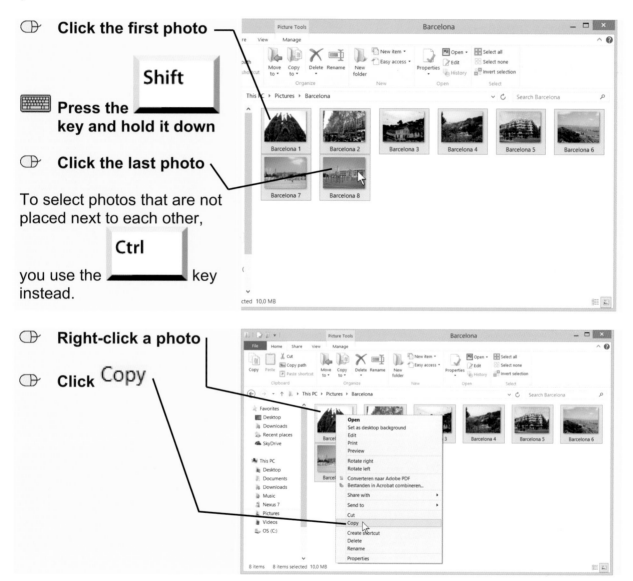

Click Nexus 7

Double-click
Internal storage
11,2 GB free of 12,2 GI

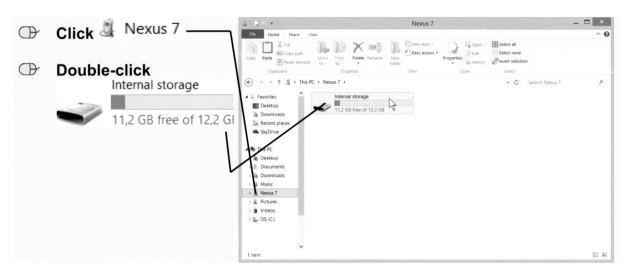

Double-click

Pictures

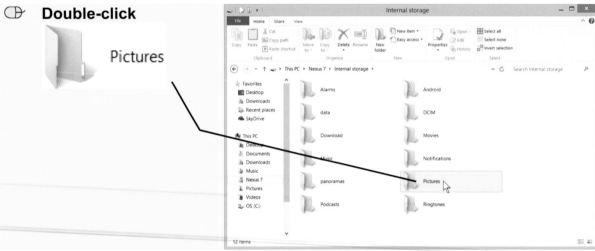

**Right-click an empty
spot in the window**

Click Paste

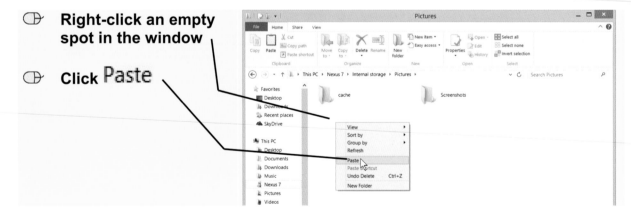

Now the photos have been
copied to your tablet:

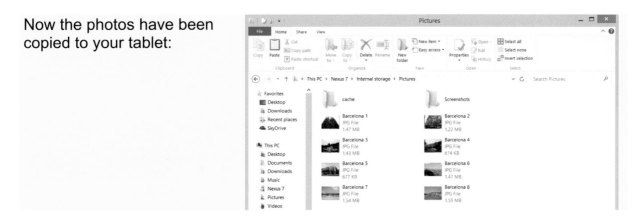

In the same way, you can copy a video file to your tablet:

👆 **Right-click the video**

👆 **Click** Copy

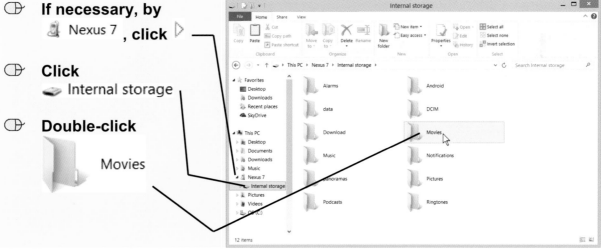

👆 **If necessary, by**
📱 Nexus 7 **, click** ▷

👆 **Click**
💾 Internal storage

👆 **Double-click**
📁 Movies

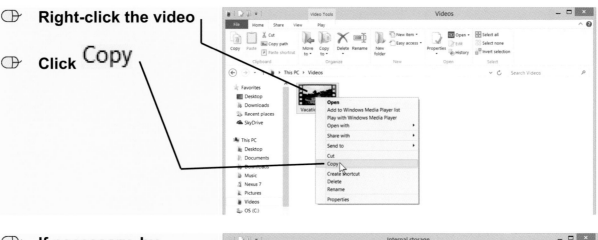

Right-click an empty spot in the window

Click Paste

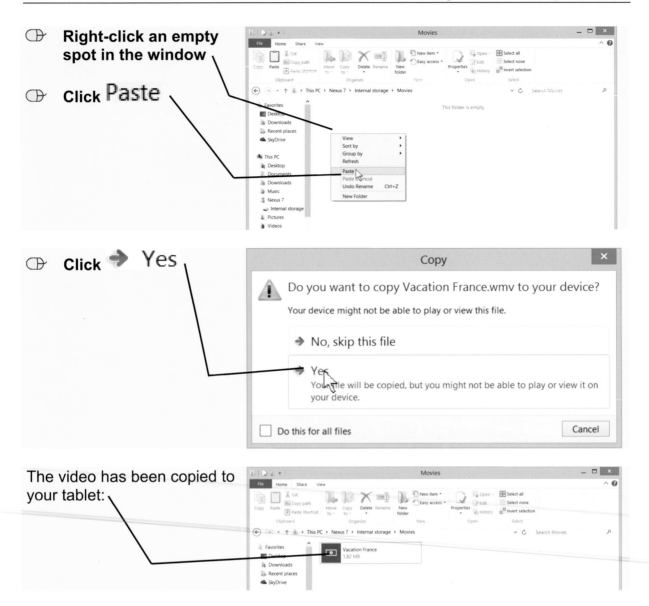

Click ➡ **Yes**

The video has been copied to your tablet:

Finally, you are going to copy some music files to your tablet. You can do this in the same way as above.

☞ **Select a number of music files**

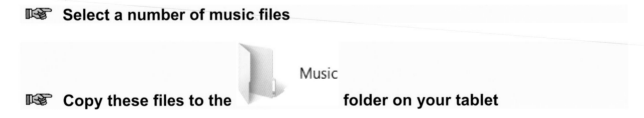

☞ **Copy these files to the** Music **folder on your tablet**

You will see this window:

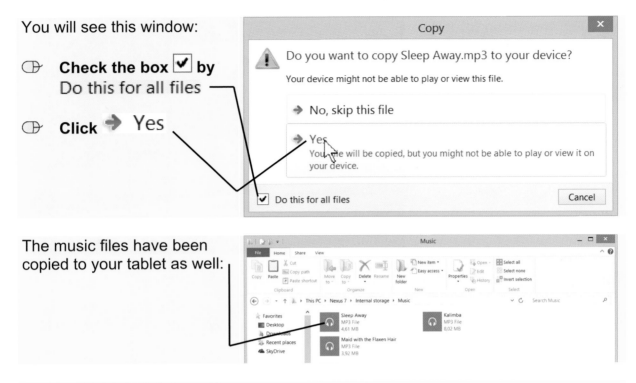

⊕ **Check the box** ☑ **by**
    Do this for all files

⊕ **Click** ➔ Yes

The music files have been copied to your tablet as well:

☞ **Close** *File Explorer* 🐾⁸

☞ **Disconnect your tablet from the computer**

Now you have stored various photo, video and music files on your tablet. In the next couple of sections you are going to use these files on your tablet.

6.6 Playing a Recorded Video

You can watch video that you have made or copied to your tablet with the same app as you have used for viewing photos, that is, the *Gallery* app.

☞ **Open the** *Gallery* **app** 🐾⁹

☞ **Tap the video folder**

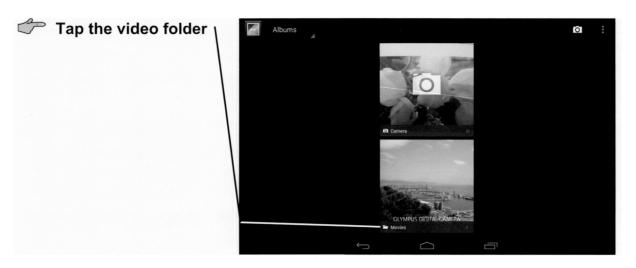

🠮 **Please note:**

If a copied video does not appear on the screen, the video file is not supported. In *section 6.5 Copying Photos, Videos and Music to Your Tablet* you can see which file formats are supported by this app.

☞ **Tap**

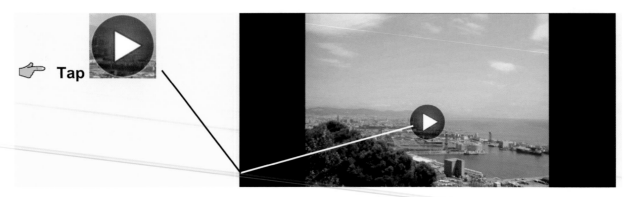

You will see this window:

☞ **Tap**

Video player

☞ **Tap Just once**

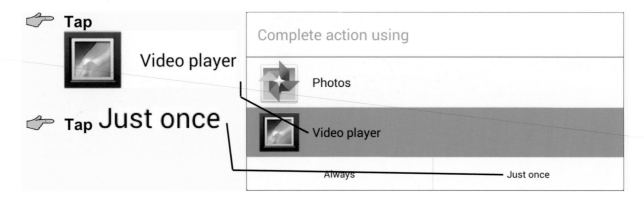

The video will be played full-screen:

☞ **Tap the image**

With the ⏸ button you can pause playback:

With the slider ⬤ you can go rewind or fast forward:

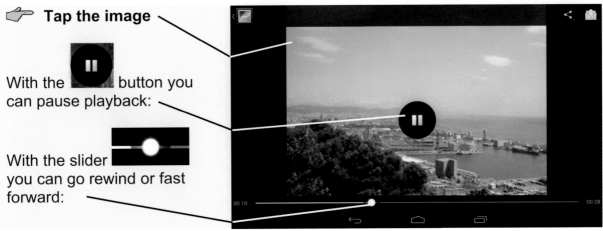

☞ **Go back to the Home screen** 👣²

💡 **Tip**

Delete a video

This is how you delete the video on your tablet:

☞ **Tap the video**

☞ **Tap** ⁞

☞ **Tap Delete**

6.7 Playing Music With the Play Music App

The Google Nexus tablet is also equipped with an extensive music player called the *Play Music* app. This is how you open the app:

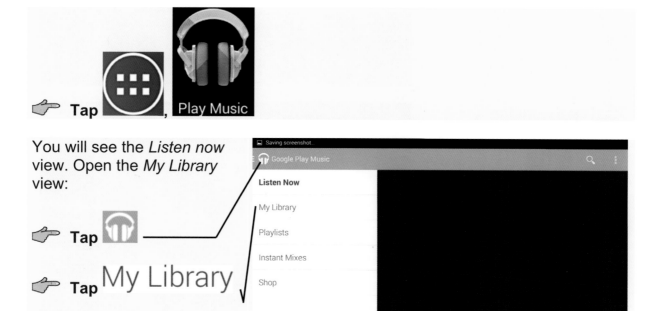

You will see the *Listen now* view. Open the *My Library* view:

☞ **Tap** 🎧

☞ **Tap** My Library

🩹 HELP! I see a different window.

If this is the first time you open *Play Music* you may see a login screen. This is what you need to do next:

☞ **Tap your account**

If you want to add a new account, tap

Add account.

Then enter the required data.

You will see a view per artist:

☞ **Tap an artist**

☞ **Tap the image**

You will see three buttons:

To view the other buttons:

☞ **Drag the lowest bar upwards**

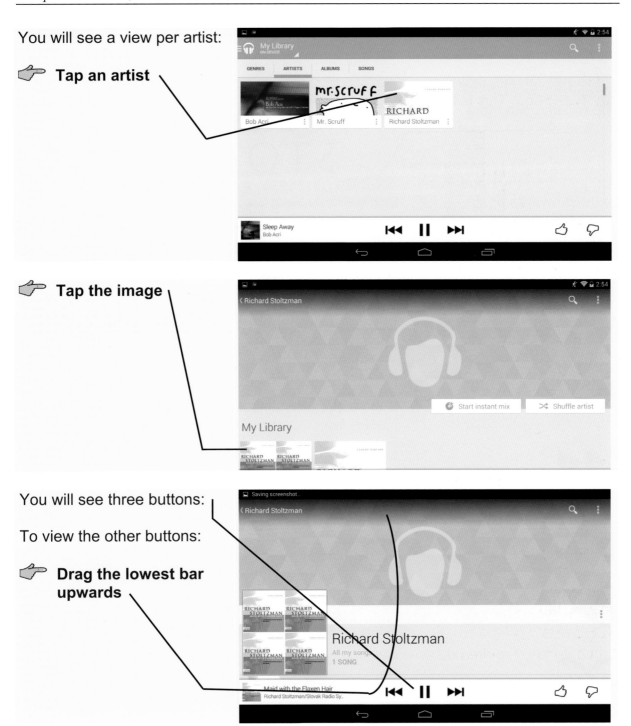

You will see the image on a full screen: ————

At the bottom of the screen you will find two more options: ————

To return to the previous view you just drag the uppermost bar downwards again.

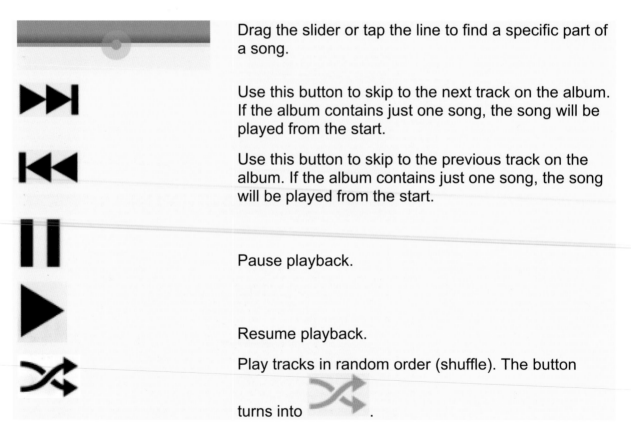

This is what the control buttons do:

	Drag the slider or tap the line to find a specific part of a song.
	Use this button to skip to the next track on the album. If the album contains just one song, the song will be played from the start.
	Use this button to skip to the previous track on the album. If the album contains just one song, the song will be played from the start.
	Pause playback.
	Resume playback.
	Play tracks in random order (shuffle). The button turns into [image].

Repeat:
- tap once: all tracks on the album will be repeated.

  The button turns into 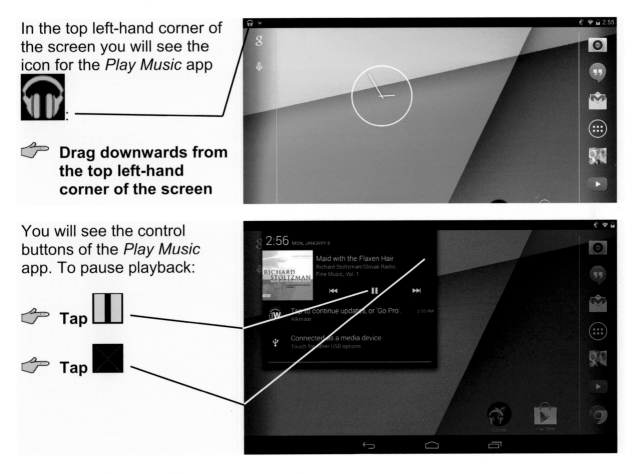 .
- tap twice: the current track will be repeated. The

  button turns into .

During playback you can quit the *Play Music* app and do something else on your tablet:

☞ **Go back to the Home screen** ²

The music will still be played. In any random app you can still display the control buttons of the *Play Music* app, in the *Notifications* screen:

In the top left-hand corner of the screen you will see the icon for the *Play Music* app

:

☞ **Drag downwards from the top left-hand corner of the screen**

You will see the control buttons of the *Play Music* app. To pause playback:

☞ **Tap**

☞ **Tap**

Now you will see the Home screen again.

6.8 Creating a Playlist With the Play Music App

The *Play Music* app has a very useful function with which you can create playlists. You can add your favorite songs to a playlist and arrange them in any order you like. Then you can play this list over and over again. Open the *Play Music* app once more:

☞ **Open the** *Play Music* **app** ✂✂**9**

You will still see the screen with the last song you played. Go back to the app's Home screen:

In the top left-hand corner of the screen:

☞ **Tap**

Maid with the Flaxen Hair
Richard Stoltzman/Slovak Radio S

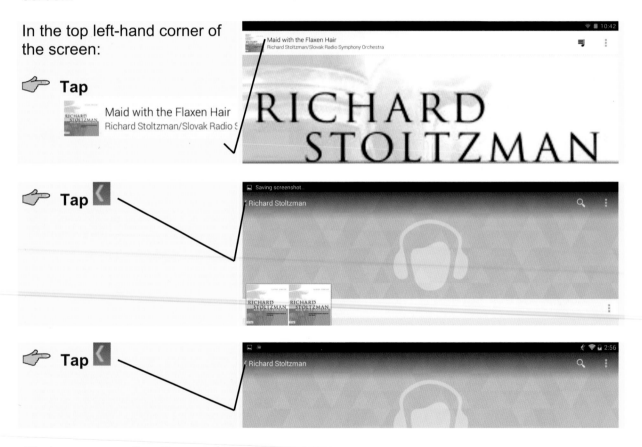

☞ **Tap** ❮

☞ **Tap** ❮

First, you open the *Songs* view:

☞ **Tap SONGS**

By the desired song,

tap

Tap Add to playlist

Tap New playlist

Type a name, for example: My favorite songs

Tap OK

Take a look at the playlist:

Tap

Tap Playlists

You will see the playlist you have just created:

☞ **Tap your playlist**

The playlist below has been automatically created by the *Play Music* app:

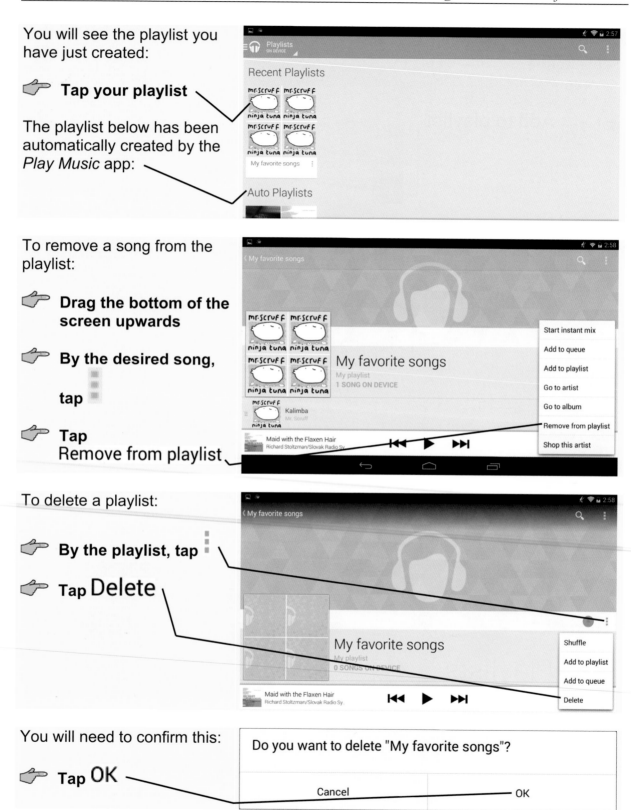

To remove a song from the playlist:

☞ **Drag the bottom of the screen upwards**

☞ **By the desired song, tap** ⦙

☞ **Tap** Remove from playlist

To delete a playlist:

☞ **By the playlist, tap** ⦙

☞ **Tap** Delete

You will need to confirm this:

☞ **Tap** OK

Do you want to delete "My favorite songs"?

Cancel   OK

💡 Tip

Delete songs

You can always delete songs from your tablet using *File Explorer* on your computer. But you can also delete them with the *Play Music* app. Here is how you do that:

☞ **By the desired song,**

  tap

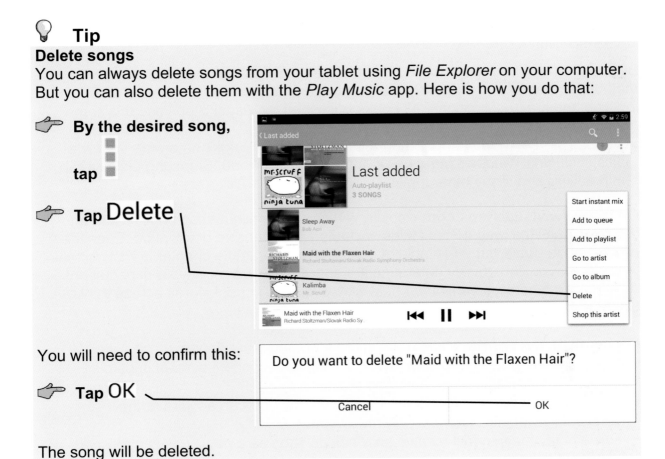

☞ **Tap** Delete

You will need to confirm this:

Do you want to delete "Maid with the Flaxen Hair"?

☞ **Tap** OK

Cancel   OK

The song will be deleted.

You have nearly reached the end of this book. In this book you have learned how to work with the Google Nexus tablet. In the *Tips* at the end of this chapter you will find some additional options you can use with the apps for photos, videos and music. Then you can start using other apps and discover even more features of this handy tablet.

6.9 Visual Steps Website

By now we hope you have noticed that the Visual Steps method is an excellent method for quickly and efficiently learning more about tablets, computers and other devices and their applications. All books published by Visual Steps use this same method.

In various series, we have published a large number of books on a wide variety of topics, including *Windows, Mac OS X,* the iPad, the iPhone*,* Samsung Galaxy Tab, photo editing and many other topics.

On the **www.visualsteps.com** website you can click the Catalog page to find an overview of all the Visual Steps titles, including an extensive description. Each title allows you to preview the full table of contents and a sample chapter in PDF format. In this way, you can quickly determine if a specific title will meet your expectations. All titles can be ordered online and are also available in bookstores across the USA, Canada, United Kingdom, Australia and New Zealand.

Furthermore, the website offers many extras, among other things:
- free computer guides and booklets (PDF files) covering all sorts of subjects;
- frequently asked questions and their answers;
- information on the free Computer Certificate that you can acquire at the certificate's website **www.ccforseniors.com**;
- a free notify-me service: receive an email as soon as a new book is published.

There is far more to learn. Visual Steps offers lots of other books on computer-related subjects. And remember: each Visual Steps book has been written using the same step-by-step method with screen shots illustrating every step.

6.10 Background Information

Dictionary

Album	The name of a folder on your tablet, containing photos or videos.
Convert	To transfer data from one file format to another.
File Explorer	A *Windows* program with which you can manage your files.
Gallery	An app for viewing photos and videos on your Google Nexus tablet.
Play Music	An app for listening to music on your Google Nexus tablet.
Playlist	A collection of songs, arranged in a certain order.
Queue	In the *Play Music* app the songs are lined up in a queue. They are set up in the order in which they will be played. You can add and delete songs from a queue.
Shuffle	Playing songs in random order.
Slideshow	An automatic display of a collection of images.
Zoom in	Take a closer look.
Zoom out	Look at something from a distance.

Source: Google Nexus tablet User Guide, Wikipedia

6.11 Tips

 Tip

Use a photo as wallpaper
You can also use one of your own photos as a background (wallpaper) for the Home screen. Here is how you do that:

☞ **Tap a photo**

☞ **Tap** ▣

☞ **Tap** Set picture as

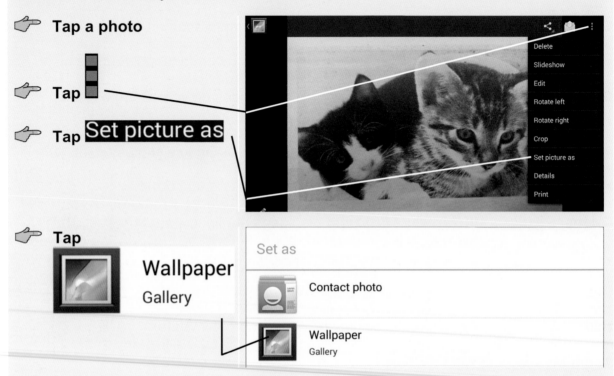

☞ **Tap**
  Wallpaper
  Gallery

Select the part of the photo you want to use. You do this by dragging the borders of the blue frame:

☞ **If necessary, drag the picture**

☞ **Tap**
  ✓ **SET WALLPAPER**

- Continue on the next page -

You can also change the background through the *Settings* screen:

☞   **Open the *Settings* screen** ✌³

👉 **Tap** ⚙ **Display**, **Wallpaper**

👉 **Tap the desired option**

👉 **Tap the desired background**

💡   **Tip**
Link a photo to a contact
In the same way you can add a photo to one of your contacts:

👉 **Tap a photo**

👉 **Tap** ⋮, **Set picture as**

👉 **Tap** **Contact photo**

👉 **Tap the desired contact**

👉 **Tap Just once**

Complete action using

🎴 Crop photo

🖼️ Crop picture

Always   Just once

- Continue on the next page -

Select the part of the photo that you want to use. You do this by dragging the frame:

☞ **Drag the frame**

If you are satisfied with the photo:

☞ **Tap**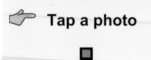

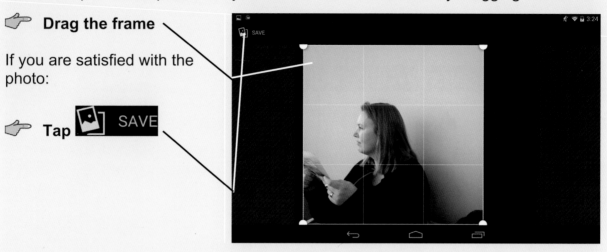

Now the photo has been added to this contact's information.

💡 **Tip**
Photo editing
The *Gallery* app comes with an assortment of photo editing options. For instance, you can rotate or crop a photo. You can also manually adjust the colors and exposure using automatic enhancement or by applying various effects.

☞ **Tap a photo**

☞ **Tap** ▮

You can rotate the photo to the left or to the right:

If you want to edit the photo:

☞ **Tap** Edit

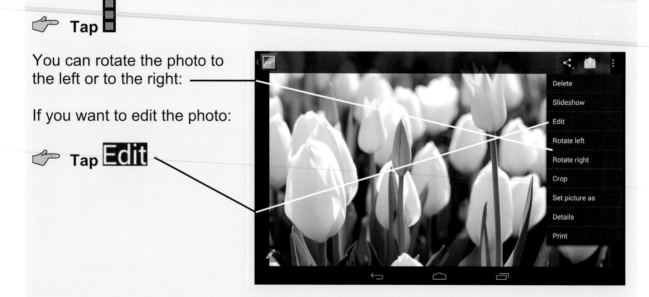

- Continue on the next page -

You will see various editing options:

 : apply an effect.

 : select a frame.

 : crop a photo.

 : various options for adjusting colors, exposure, contrast, etcetera.

You can undo the changes

with :

Use the  button to save an edited photo:

The photo will be saved separately along with the original photo.

💡 **Tip**

Delete an album from the Gallery

In the *Gallery* app you can delete photos and videos, one by one. But you can also delete an entire album at once:

☞ **Tap your finger gently on an album until you**

see 🗑 **at the top of the screen**

☞ **Tap** 🗑

You will need to confirm this:

☞ **Tap**

💡 **Tip**

Music in the queue

By adding songs to the queue, the songs will be played in the order in which you have arranged them. This is how you add a song to a queue:

☞ **Select the *Songs* view** 👣13

👉 **By the desired song, tap** ⋮

👉 **Tap** # Add to queue

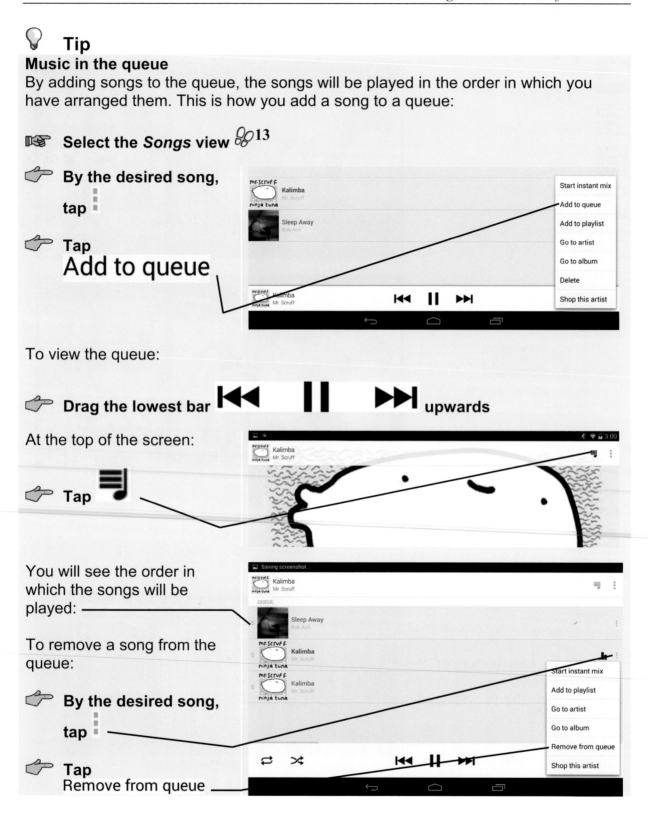

To view the queue:

👉 **Drag the lowest bar** ⏮ ⏸ ⏭ **upwards**

At the top of the screen:

👉 **Tap** 🎵

You will see the order in which the songs will be played:

To remove a song from the queue:

👉 **By the desired song, tap** ⋮

👉 **Tap** Remove from queue

Appendix A. How Do I Do That Again?

The actions in this book are marked with footsteps: 𝓫𝓫1
If you have forgotten how to do something, you can read how to do it again by finding the corresponding number in the list below.

𝓫𝓫1 **Unlock or turn on the tablet**
Unlock:
- Briefly press the power button

- Place your finger on the screen, or on

- Drag the padlock icon to the edge of the circle

Turn on:
- Press the power button until you see the *Google* logo

𝓫𝓫2 **Go back to the Home screen**
- Tap

𝓫𝓫3 **Open the *Settings* screen**
- Drag downwards from the top right-hand corner of the screen

- Tap SETTINGS

𝓫𝓫4 **Download and install an app**
Free app:
- Tap the app

- Tap INSTALL

- Tap ACCEPT

Paid app:
- Tap the app

- Tap 0.99 (the amount may differ)

- Tap ACCEPT

- Tap BUY

- Type your password

- Tap CONFIRM

𝓫𝓫5 **Lock or turn off the tablet**
Lock:
- Briefly press the power button

Turn off:
- Press the power button a while longer

- Tap ⏻ Power off

- Tap OK

6 Go to another tab in *Chrome*
- Tap the tab, for example

7 Add a contact

- Tap
- Tap OK
- Type the information for this contact
- Tap ✓ DONE

8 Close a window on computer
- Click ✕

9 Open an app
- Tap
- Tap the app

10 Move an app to another page
- Press your finger on the app
- Drag the app to the border of the screen

When you see the other page:
- Release the app

11 Remove an app from the Home screen
- Press your finger on the app
- Drag the app to ⊠
- Release the app

12 Open a photo in *Gallery*
- Tap an album with photos
- Tap a photo

13 Select *Songs* view in the *Play Music* app
- If necessary, tap ❮ a couple of times
- Tap SONGS

14 Make a picture
- Point the camera towards the object you want to photograph

- Tap

Appendix B. Index